IN HONOR OF
WOMEN

IN HONOR OF WOMEN

A Revolutionary Approach to Preventing
Breast Cancer and Other Diseases

STELLA TOGO CRAWLEY

Ballantine Books · New York

A Ballantine Book
Published by The Ballantine Publishing Group

The intent of this book is to offer information of a general nature to help you attain emotional and physical well-being. The author of this book does not dispense medical advice nor recommend the use of any specific technique as a form of treatment for physical or emotional problems. The information in this book is not intended—either directly or indirectly—to be a substitute for consulting your physician. Any attempt to diagnose or treat an illness should come under the direction of a medical professional.

The inclusion of American Cancer Society breast self-examination guidelines does not constitute support or endorsement by the American Cancer Society of the concepts, theories, or conclusions presented by the author.

http://www.randomhouse.com

Library of Congress Catalog Card Number: 98-96011

ISBN: 0-345-42513-8

Book design: Sara Patton Book Production Services

Cover design: Julia Ryan, Dunn & Associates

Manufactured in the United States of America

First Ballantine Books Trade Edition: May 1998
10 9 8 7 6 5 4 3 2 1

Dedication

I dedicate this book to my little prince and princess, Christopher and Arianna. You are the stars in my life. May the brilliance of your spirits dance into a future filled with self-love, joy, and peace.

And to all the children in the world who have lost a mother to breast cancer: May you be blessed with an abundance of love, comfort, strength, and wisdom.

In honor of all the women of the world: May we discover, one day soon, a world free of self-criticism and guilt, a space where we are happy to truly honor ourselves and cater to the desires of our hearts, a time when the divine feminine spirit is realized as being far bigger than any disease.

In memory of the women who have died of breast cancer, the angels who once walked the earth: May you rest in peace and know you have not died in vain. I honor your voices and your clear message.

To the many families who have lost a beloved to breast cancer: May your hearts be consoled.

Contents

Contents

Contents

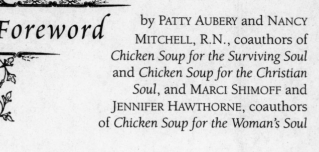

Foreword

by PATTY AUBERY and NANCY MITCHELL, R.N., coauthors of *Chicken Soup for the Surviving Soul* and *Chicken Soup for the Christian Soul*, and MARCI SHIMOFF and JENNIFER HAWTHORNE, coauthors of *Chicken Soup for the Woman's Soul*

In a world where there is so much fear based on a disease that seems so out of control, we welcome the insight that is shared within this book. *In Honor of Women* offers a different angle on breast cancer, one that empowers women to feel in control. It not only eases fear, but it gives hope for a brighter future.

Women as a whole are passionate about self-help. Our healing abilities are clearly what pave the way for others and our future generations. How proud we are to live in a time when so much healing is taking place.

We are honored to preface the following material, as it inspires women to discover self-love and a higher sense of self-esteem. *In Honor of Women* is an important work that restores a deep sense of confidence in women. We personally are grateful to Stella Togo Crawley for identifying the strength in women and reminding us of our inner light. Let us move forward as our spirit is elevated to new heights!

—SPRING 1998

Acknowledgments

Alive is the American dream that my parents, Grace Dicillo Togo and Frank Togo, were inspired by as they crossed the Atlantic from Italy in the late 1950s. With little to call their own, their vision of providing a brighter future for their children was the dream of a lifetime. They instilled in me the ability to dream and to believe in myself. The greatest gift they gave me, in addition to my life, is the passion and inner strength that comes from having a dream. I thank you for all the sacrifices you made along the way in raising me to be the individual I am today. I thank you for your unconditional love and support, for being there to care for my children during my recovery, and for believing in me.

A time-intensive project like this book would not have been possible without the emotional and financial support I received from my loving husband, John Crawley Jr. Faced with a life-threatening disease, I was deeply empowered by your love, comfort, and devotion. I thank you for all the times you sat through doctor's appointments; the many hours you spent in hospital lobbies waiting alone, praying for me; and for taking care of the children so I could spend countless hours researching and developing this project.

Thanks to my children, Christopher and Arianna, for all the times you played quietly so that Mom could work. The precious moments of hearing your little voices from the other room firmly declare, "I love you, Mom," beautifully reminded me of how blessed I am to be *so* loved.

Thanks to my brothers, Giorgio and Dominic Togo, for your loving support and for being there when I needed a friend. You are more like brothers than uncles to my children. I love you dearly.

Pop Pop (John P. Crawley Sr.), thank you for your support and sense of humor. Together with your wife, Mary Crawley, you raised nine fantastic individuals. To all the Crawleys, I am proud to be part of this wonderful family. Special thanks to Mary Crawley Cooper for your enthusiasm and loving support.

I send my deep, heartfelt gratitude to my team of doctors and people who joined me as partners in my healing: Dr. Kammerman, you literally saved my life by paying attention to a lump that could have easily been misdiagnosed. My surgeons, Dr. West and Dr. Kent, you listened to my needs and went far beyond the call of duty to assist me in my recovery. My oncologist, Dr. Glaspy, I appreciate your jovial attitude and attending to my needs. My biochemist, Dr. Rodino, you were the angel who appeared to guide me back to health; thank you for all your nutritional programs, supplements, and insights on well-being. Thanks to Dr. Chen, my acupuncturist, for assisting me during chemotherapy; to Dr. Campbell, my chiropractor, for assisting me in preparing for all of my surgeries; and to each staff member in the doctors' offices, for playing a significant role in communicating my needs and concerns. And special thanks to Dr. Anzaldo and your wonderful staff for your loving support!

Jean Sedbrook, a survivor and volunteer for the Breast Care Center (Orange, California), your guidance, love, and support eased my concerns significantly. A special thanks to Cheryll Estes from Dr. Rodino's office. Pindey Shahi, my masseur, your loving energy strengthens my sense of well-being; thank you for your beautiful prayer contribution. And appreciation to Dr. Dennis Gowans and Dr. Wayne Hart for your loving support.

Thanks to the many friends and neighbors who believed in me and supported me throughout the five years it took for this book to come to fruition: Dan Jurich, an engineer and brilliant teacher who makes technical learning a breeze (and enjoyable!), thanks for your countless hours helping me finalize and prepare the materials for my editor. The Rinella family, I am grateful for your friendship and support. My best friend, Linda Phelan, thank you for your unconditional love and amazing support! I am truly blessed by your friendship. Thank you, Elle Keith, for your love, wisdom, and guidance. To all our wonderful and loving friends at Farmers Insurance Group, I appreciate your loving thoughts and prayers. And thanks to my dear friends, with whom I love to celebrate life: Barbara and Jerry Levitt, Pinky and Armando Fernandez, Geneva and Tim Roe, MaryEllen and Jim Pappas, Wendy and Steve Kelly, Lenda and Mark Heineman.

My sincerest gratitude goes to all of the brilliant authors who took time out of their busy schedules to share their thoughts: Marianne Williamson; Louise L. Hay; Dr. Bernie Siegel; Mark Victor Hansen; Jack Canfield; Patty Aubery; Nancy Mitchell, R.N.; Jennifer Hawthorne; and Marci Shimoff. Thank you, Kisma Stepanich, author of *Sister Moon Lodge*, for your wonderful insight. Special thanks to Dan Poynter, author of *The Self-Publishing Manual*, for your great recommendations.

To Teresa Spohn, marketing director for the Canfield Group: a special thanks for your assistance. Thanks to Julie Barnes, Mark Victor Hansen's former personal assistant, for your support and assistance.

To my mentor, Dottie Walters, author of *Speak and Grow Rich* and *Never Underestimate the Selling Power of a Woman*, the first book ever written by a woman for women in sales. I am deeply grateful for your tremendous knowledge, expertise, and most of all your encouraging words.

To Michael Hutchison at Ambassador Management Group, many thanks for assisting me in developing a series of future books and expanding my vision. Thanks for seeing the value in this work and for all of your support and marketing expertise.

A world of thanks to Robert Wisneski, at The Helfrich Company, for putting me in contact with Michael Hutchison, who is also the former vice president of sales and marketing for Tony Robbins. I will always treasure my connection with you.

To one of my dearest friends and a woman who has had a profound impact on my life since the day we met, Mimi Michael: I thank you for working with me and inspiring me to learn to honor myself and to receive—truly an invaluable lesson!

A special thanks to all the women I interviewed for my personal study, and to the men and women who contributed their expertise and personal stories: Saskia R. J. Thiadens, R.N., president of the National Lymphedema Network; JoAnn Rovig, co-founder of the Northwest Lymphedema Center; Janie Gabbett-Lee, friend and editor; Barbara Anabo, foundation director of the Breast Care Center and friend; and Gerry Stacy, co-founder of Y-ME Orange County.

A very special thank you to Phyllis Clark, Nordstrom Orange County Regional Prosthesis Coordinator; Nancy Knoble; Barbara Scott; Joy Escoe; Barri Carian; Micki Voisard; Dr. Benjamin Anderson, assistant professor of surgical oncology for the University of Washington; Dr. Ernis Bodai, chief of surgery at Kaiser Permanente Sacramento; Leslie Goldman at Enchanted Garden; and Elaine Jensen at Richard's Hair Design. A special thanks goes to the American Cancer Society for permission to include the information on breast self-examination, a vital section of this book. Sue Parker, thank you for your lovely prayer. Thank you, *Timothy*, for your suggestions and insight on the publication of this book.

Many thanks to Patricia McDade, the creator of The Entrepreneurial Edge, for teaching and showing me how to get out of my own way!!! I love you dearly.

I wish to acknowledge four incredible individuals who poured their hearts and souls into the production of the first edition of this book. Sara Patton, whose beautiful spirit is reflected in the interior design of this book. Julia Ryan, who heard the spiritual voice behind the message and brought it to life in the form of a gorgeous cover. I love you both dearly. Marty and Diane Gilliland, I thank you for all your assistance and the fine quality of the first printing.

To my second and powerful team of outstanding professionals who are making it possible to get this message to women all over the world, thank you for touching my heart with your enthusiasm and commitment to this project.

My deepest gratitude goes to my agent, Meredith Bernstein, for her sense of timing in introducing me to the folks at Ballantine Books within a week of receiving her copy. To Maureen O'Neal, my editor at Ballantine Books, you have made my dream come true. Thank you for the privilege of publishing this work with you and the many brilliant souls at Ballantine who are blessed for their hard work. Thanks to you, many lives will be touched as a result of your efforts.

To Teri Love, my personal assistant, thank you for being such a gift in my life.

I thank every individual who has blessed this work long before it took its final form. It would be easy to fill another book just expressing all of the gratitude that fills my heart. I am truly grateful for all that I have received. May every one of you receive a thousandfold the blessings you have given me.

Cure Breast Cancer Stamp

On August 13, 1997, President Clinton signed legislation co-sponsored by Senator Feinstein to create a breast cancer research stamp. The law directs the U.S. Postal Service to create a special first-class postage stamp priced at up to 25 percent above the cost of a regular first-class stamp to be purchased voluntarily by the public. Proceeds from funds raised by the stamp will be directed to breast cancer research.

The idea of the breast cancer research stamp originated in California from Dr. "Ernie" Bodai, chief of surgery at Kaiser Permanente in Sacramento, California, who has treated more than 1,500 women with breast cancer.

Under the Stamp Out Breast Cancer legislation:

+ The Postal Service will establish a special rate of postage for first-class mail, not to exceed 25 percent of the first-class rate, as an alternate to the regular first-class postage. The additional sum would be contributed to breast cancer research.
+ The rate would be determined in part by the Postal Service to cover administrative costs, and the remainder by the Governors of the Postal Service.

+ Seventy percent of the funds raised would fund breast cancer research at NIH and 30 percent of the funds raised would go to breast cancer research at DoD.
+ These funds cannot be used to offset the government's regular allocations.
+ The Postal Service would provide the stamp within a year from the date of enactment.
+ Within three months prior to the stamp's second-year anniversary, the Bill requires the Comptroller General to evaluate the effectiveness and the appropriateness of this method of fundraising and report its findings to Congress.

If only 10 percent of all first-class stamp users purchased the breast cancer research stamp, approximately $60 million additional dollars could be raised for breast cancer each year. A 50 percent buy rate would yield $300 million annually, nearly matching the entire NIH budget. The research stamp is a way to raise funds to find a cure for breast cancer without raising new taxes or taking scarce research dollars from other programs. For true success of this program, it is imperative that everyone use the stamp as it becomes available. CBC has one goal: to cease to exist. Then the dream of Dr. Bodai will be realized. The plan is to have four different designs of stamps: 1) one feminine design, 2) one design that includes women of color, 3) a research stamp, and 4) a family portrait as a final design representing the families that are affected by breast cancer. Each of these designs will be created by women. The following is a sample of what a research stamp may look like.

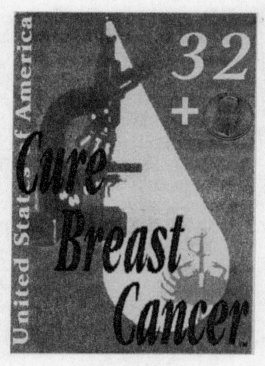

CALL (916) 973-6120

Introduction

This book gives voice to the tremendous unconscious dis-ease of women, and a disease that has plagued them for many generations. Herein lies a revolutionary approach to preventing breast cancer and a better understanding of the rhyme and reason to its madness.

In the ten years of the Vietnam War, 54,000 U.S. soldiers died. During that same period, 330,000 women lost their lives to breast cancer. Currently, 2.6 million women are living with this disease. It is estimated that 180,200 women were diagnosed in 1997. One woman dies of breast cancer every twelve minutes—estimated at 43,900 deaths in 1997 alone.

Researchers speculate that the increase in the incidence of breast cancer since 1940 may be due to the rising prevalence of breast cancer risk factors, such as *the modern reproductive patterns of women having fewer children and delaying their first childbirth until a later age* (American Cancer Society, *Cancer Facts and Figures,* 1997).

It was this information that inspired me, as a survivor, to do my own personal study and identify other possible patterns. *In Honor of Women* takes a close look at ten specific emotional and psychological patterns, or "commonalities," of more than two hundred breast cancer survivors. Although women today are mothering fewer children, overmothering and overachieving seem to be common threads among women who have breast cancer. Many of the commonalities are a result of beliefs that have been passed on through generations.

It is important to recognize that the purpose of bringing forth this information is to *empower women*, and identify ways in which we may learn to honor ourselves and therefore gain a higher sense of self-esteem and self-worth. There seems to be a false sense of heroism based on our giving *so* much of ourselves away—whether it's to a job, a marriage, a relationship, or by simply denying the needs of the self. Many women who have been diagnosed have said, "How can this be happening to me? I give so much."

Based on my own healing and the many gifts I have received as a result, I strongly believe that this disease has delivered to us a beautiful message that has not been acknowledged by the mass consciousness.

Like many other survivors, I gave far more than I allowed myself to receive. My sense of self-worth was based on how much I was doing for others and I completely ignored my own desires and needs. My sense of "being" was overrun by all my "doing." Although I was diagnosed at thirty-two, the commonalities are the same across the board when it comes to women of various age groups. (I did, however, find some interesting indicators of why the highest percentage of women who are diagnosed are middle-aged.) The message that I have learned and embraced is to honor myself, to balance giving with receiving, to fill my cup first so that I can give tirelessly and effortlessly, and to "be" in the moment instead of in the "next."

The spiritual meaning of breast cancer is giving away our divine feminine and nurturing self. During my five years of research and development for this book, I found that women who are diagnosed and begin to truly honor themselves have a better chance of survival than those who don't. Within these pages you will find stories written by survivors that clearly outline and support these findings. And women who fear getting this disease have an opportunity to feel more in control, as fear itself has a chapter of its own.

This book is about the divine feminine spirit, and the power and strength we are born with.

Women are the link between Spirit and life, yet there is so much dis-ease within our hearts. It is time to shed the guilt, the "shoulds," the "coulds," and the "woulds"—the same way a snake sheds its skin. It is time to reclaim our divinity and wear it like a new outfit. Our hearts deserve to be heard and to be happy.

Whether you are a woman who fears breast cancer, has had breast cancer, knows someone who has been diagnosed, or have been recently diagnosed, you will find a significant amount of information—all in the name of honoring yourself. Learn what it means to honor yourself and integrate it in your daily life using "101 Ways to Honor Yourself as a Woman" (presented in Chapter 8).

Although breast cancer appears to be an epidemic, it is not. I feel that *women are bigger than breast cancer*. If we understand the commonalities and how dis-ease manifests symptoms in the body, we may be able to prevent ourselves from developing it and other diseases. The information and strategies this book presents have immediate application for those who seek fulfillment and love in their lives. Many women have tearfully shared their gratitude for identifying the spirit and love that mirrors them within these pages.

Best of all, this book offers hope. Hope that more women will embrace their own hearts and desires as

they have for others, therefore creating new core beliefs for their daughters and generations to come.
Hope that breast cancer will cease to exist as a result
of honoring ourselves and being honored by our
world. Hope that both men and women all over the
world will understand the link between our spirit,
mind, and body. If we identify with our spirit, we
have a better chance of understanding our mind and
the healing that occurs within the body. Finally, *In
Honor of Women* offers hope that languaging such as
"the fight against breast cancer" will soon shift to "the
healing of breast cancer" . . . *for breast cancer is merely
a symptom of what is occurring with the women of the
world.*

It is my love and passion for life that inspired me
to write this book, and my love for women and
humankind that inspired me to share it. I offer it as
a gift, with much love and blessings to all.

—STELLA TOGO CRAWLEY
SPRING 1997

A Special Prayer

In Honor of Women

We give great thanks for this opportunity to
come together.

We come seeking the Truth and ask that it be
given in a manner that we might understand.

We commit to using the information gathered
here only for the highest good and only in
the name of love.

We acknowledge that we are always surrounded
by the forces of love, light, wisdom, and
healing, and nothing else may enter.

May we radiate the loving, nurturing power
of the divine feminine spirit more fully in
our lives and in the world.

—MIMI MICHAEL

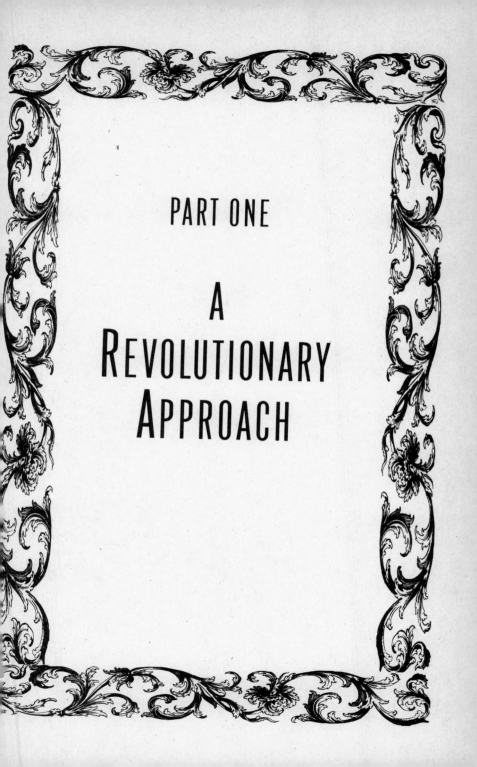

PART ONE

A
REVOLUTIONARY
APPROACH

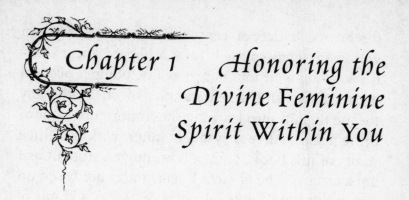

Chapter 1   *Honoring the Divine Feminine Spirit Within You*

As a child, I remember dancing with my grand-mother and learning to waltz. Every step was a conscious effort to keep up with the tempo and her instructions. At times I thought I'd never learn. She would constantly remind me to look at her face and not her feet. Once I focused on looking at her face, I had no choice but to feel the music. Soon the music began to magically move my feet into the proper steps. Before long I grew to love the waltz and looked forward to every time we danced. I was so carried by the music that I'd literally forget all about my feet! I'd find myself laughing with her as we moved gracefully through the house. I loved gliding into each movement and the freedom it evoked within me.

This is one of my fondest childhood memories, and one I can easily relate to today as I have been learning a new dance, a dance that requires the focus of the heart and not just the mind. While listening to my heartbeat as the tempo in music, I have discovered a deeper sense of self and a freedom within my own spirit. It took a breast cancer diagnosis, along with four surgeries (including a bilateral mastectomy) and seven months of chemotherapy for me to shift into learning the importance of honoring myself. After six years of inner work and three drafts of this book, I am still as much a student as I am a teacher. The choices I make today are based on the multitude of gifts I have received as a result of my experience. I share these gifts as the steps to a new dance, a new way of life, one that may prevent women from receiving a diagnosis of breast cancer and possibly other diseases.

It had been about a year since my diagnosis when I began my work with Mimi Michael, one of the most spiritual and loving women I know. My very first meeting with Mimi began a process of tremendous inner growth. Little did I know the fullness and abundance of gifts I would receive as a direct result of our time together. In a bookstore, pushing my daughter Arianna in a stroller, I noticed Mimi for the first time as she walked past me. I can't tell you why, but I instinctively knew I had to speak to her. Within minutes, we were engaged in a powerful conversation that lasted an hour and a half. Arianna, amazingly, reflected my peacefulness, and remained unusually content. It was as though time stood still, and all the chaos of the outside world took a break. I had never experienced self-realization as I did that moment.

It was here that I first heard the words "divine feminine spirit." Chills swept though my body as I, for the very first time, began to look at a deeper sense of self. Those three words sounded as a distant bell, plunging me into years of self-discovery. I am honored to have learned and processed the meaning of those words—not only for my own awakening, but for the awakening of women everywhere.

Residing within every man and every woman are the male spirit and the feminine spirit, much like the right brain and the left brain. The two spirits are very different, and it is important to distinguish the qualities that each provide so we can better understand their purpose. In understanding their purpose, we are then able to create balance in our lives and in our world.

The divine male spirit wields the sword while the divine feminine spirit carries the wand. The masculine spirit represents the physical sense of things, the provider, the protector, and the gifts of *doing* and *giving*. The feminine spirit represents all that comes from the heart, such as feelings, spiritualism, nurturing, healing, love, as well as the gifts of *being* and *receiving*.

Although every human being is blessed with all

of these gifts, I believe that women on a mass consciousness level have never been taught to honor the divine feminine spirit within. Therefore we are not in balance with our own power. *No one is at fault for this, for it is the evolution of humankind that has brought us thus far.*

For the most part, women (including myself) have learned to wield the sword without the balance of the wand. We know what it's like to live within the male spirit of *doing*, yet the very core of our being is to *be* and to *receive* first. For example, a woman cannot give life without receiving a seed. As women, we have learned to base our self-worth on what we have accomplished according to the male spirit. It is time to reclaim our self-worth and inner power through the divine feminine spirit.

The divine feminine spirit is where we hold our sacredness. It is the feminine aspect of the Divine, of God. This is where all of creation originates and, as women, we are in direct line with the Infinite Creator. It is no coincidence that Earth is often referred to as Mother Earth, because someone or something is born here every second of every day! Do you know just how sacred women are? *We are the link between Spirit and life!* If the earth was left with one woman and billions of men, our species would die. Yet, reverse this scenario, with one man and many women, and the species lives on! Women represent life, and give life to everything they touch.

In my workshops I am often asked by women who have not been able to bear children and/or have had hysterectomies how this relates to them. Every woman possesses within the cells of her body the blueprint of all the women before her. You need not bear a child or even have a womb to know that you are equally divine.

The process of reconnecting with the divine feminine spirit is trusting our inner sense of knowing and allowing it to guide us. There is great wisdom within us, just waiting to be discovered. It is simply a matter of listening to our inner voice. Many of the answers we seek in the outside world are truly found *within* our hearts. Yet, many of us were taught early on that others know what is best for us, and we unconsciously deny ourselves the wisdom of our own knowledge. The more we allow ourselves to trust and *focus* on our own voice, the more empowered we become. This is how we begin to receive abundance on all levels.

If you are like most women, giving is far easier and more comfortable than receiving. It is so easy to give to others. In fact, I have discovered that the whole concept of receiving is extremely foreign to most women. It's interesting to me that "receiving" is a word not often used in relation to women at all.

I am not certain how it has come about, but somehow women have learned to feel guilty for taking care of themselves. How dare we take time solely for our own purpose? We seem to be so trapped by all of our To Do lists, and all that we *should* do, that we lose sight of who we are.

In fact, how often do we ignore our own needs so we can take care of everyone and everything else? I personally remember days when I honestly forgot to eat lunch because I was so busy! *There seems to be a false sense of heroism based on how much we do, regardless of what it costs us.*

Many women who identify with this feel there is something missing in their life. Yet it is far too scary to stop and find out what is missing, for fear of the unknown. So, we stay busy and wish the feeling away. Of course, we are happy to be of service to those who need us, and we truly believe in our hearts that our joy comes from doing and giving. However, we run the risk of living in the "next," and time suddenly rushes by. Living in the male spirit as a doer and a giver, without taking the time to acknowledge what we receive, leads to a very fast-paced life with little self-love.

This is where the balance of the divine feminine spirit is so necessary. It teaches us to live within the moment and be fully aware with all of our senses; to feel total aliveness as we take notice of what we are receiving while we are doing. Honoring the feminine spirit within allows us to stop the mind from racing with thoughts of all that needs to be done.

This gives us a feeling of peacefulness as we permit ourselves to simply just *be* in the moment. For example, I can choose to truly taste the food I am nourishing my body with and be fully aware of my gratitude for each bite. I can choose to feel the sheets with which I am making the bed. I can choose to connect with people by listening with my heart and not just my ears. I can choose to be fully present in the moment so that the person I am with feels special and important. By making these choices, I am truly choosing to live in the feminine spirit at all times.

Bring forth this spirit in everything you do, and in doing so you begin to truly experience life! Become aware of how you are *being* in the moment, and you will experience more fulfillment by not having everything so neatly mapped out.

At times it is easy to believe that we have more control if we consistently plan ahead in order to avoid glitches. When challenges do occur, it can be very upsetting if we want to be in control, especially when we know we cannot govern what takes place. This is the perfect time to let go and let things be. Otherwise we can literally become consumed with stress and personal pressure trying to make sure that things never get out of control again. This is neither healthy nor realistic. Simply put, *life does not flow for those who seek control all the time.*

This is what it looks like to operate from the masculine spirit without the awareness of the feminine. A woman who feels she needs to control everything in her life carries her sword with her at all times. Believe me, I know—I carried my sword proudly for many years. It was not until I was diagnosed with breast cancer that I realized it was time to bring in the wand. *This for me was a true awakening, that living primarily in the masculine spirit serves only to destroy the feminine within.*

When there is balance with the feminine spirit, there is more trust and a knowing that there is purpose in everything that happens. There is gratitude, for we know that something much, much bigger will be shown to us. I believe that the phrase "God works in mysterious ways" is often used when things seem to work out better than we ever imagined. This is really Divine order, and it is always at work. The feminine spirit reflects this as an inner knowing, and therefore also understands that all things happen exactly as they should. Trust lives in knowing that all is well and that there is only perfection in all that occurs.

Life flows with ease for those who trust and know that everything that occurs is perfect. The need for control becomes secondary; it is no longer first and foremost in our lives.

Shortly after my diagnosis I began to do a personal study of women who had survived breast cancer. I felt there had to be a deeper meaning to all of this chaos. At times, it seemed that a day wouldn't go by without someone approaching me with another story. I kept asking myself, "Why are *so* many women getting breast cancer? What happened in my life that exposed me to getting this disease, particularly when I felt I was eating right, exercising, and living a 'normal' life?" It didn't seem right to just say, "It's the air we breathe, or the food we eat, or the environment," although I could easily accept these as possibilities. *My sense was that whatever it was, it had to be something that we (women) were not aware of, therefore we could not change it.* It was also interesting to me that breast cancer is believed to be hereditary in only five percent of the women who are diagnosed. I cannot truly explain this, but I knew I would somehow find meaning to this great mystery, and that the answer I was seeking was within me as well as in the hearts of all women.

I began to ask the women who came forth questions about their cases, and about their personal lives five to ten years prior to diagnosis—questions about their marriages, relationships, self-care, careers, and self-fulfillment. Most of the women blamed stress for their cancer. "So, what was or is the stress in your life?" I would ask.

Some women would start to cry as they shared

their painful truths about difficult marriages that ended up in divorce. Some shared their secret resentment about being the caregiver to someone they didn't wish to spend much time with in the first place, such as a verbally abusive in-law. Some were so far removed from their inner self that all that was left was to feel victimized. Some admitted that although they sensed something was deeply wrong, their egos wouldn't allow them to look at it, for fear of seeing themselves as weak. This last thought was the one that stood out the most to me, because *my* ego was really tied to looking good, completely oblivious of what that would cost me.

Regardless of the different details of each situation, there was a common thread of a general lack of self-worth, a feeling of not being good enough. With many (including myself), there was also the sense that it was easier to focus on other people and things than ourselves. The whole concept of *receiving* stopped women in their tracks. They would ask, "What do you mean, receive? What is that?" In many cases, this realization brought tears to their eyes . . . tears of gratitude, as if they were recognizing their own divinity—and being recognized as divine—*for the very first time.* Witnessing truth in their eyes left me hungry for more.

Some would laugh sarcastically while their hearts quietly yearned for a new way of being. Many welcomed the concept of their own worthiness whole-heartedly.

The more I dove into my questioning with other women, the more painful this process became for me, as I faced a little portion of myself in each of these women, thus facing my own truth. It was interesting to find myself resisting my own truth initially as part of my fear of pain and the unknown. Looking back, I now understand how normal and necessary this "growing pain" really was.

There were times when I would come home and sob at the recognition of my own pain as a reflection of the commonalities I found in other women. It was truly overwhelming to recognize the lack of self-worth in myself and in so many women. I literally mourned for months the pain that women have endured as a result of feeling "less than" or not valued.

Perhaps the most confrontive awareness was that what many of us feel has been so deep for so many generations, it has BECOME unconscious. In my opinion, it is this tremendous unconscious pain that has led so many of us to developing breast cancer and other diseases. The recognition of this, and all the commonalities with my "sisters," freed me from my own prison. The transformation that occurred was profound as I released many of my old ways of being. As a result, I began to open myself to life like never before. And I began to slowly peel away each unconscious pattern, much like peeling away the layers of an onion. The key was acknowledging these beliefs as simply old patterns, without guilt or self-blame for having them. My prayer for you is that you choose to leave behind any patterns that no longer serve you, as I did, without blaming yourself. Our truth has a way of lifting the spirit and freeing us from old patterns, so we can begin to experience inner harmony.

Although I was thirty-two years old at the time, most of the women I interviewed were between forty and fifty-five years old. In case after case, I found specific distinctions that allowed me to understand clearly what the commonalities of this disease are, regardless of age:

1. A strong need to control and have things a certain way, a lack of trust in life.
2. Overdoing, a sense of constantly having to do more, looking at the "next."
3. Overmothering, giving the feminine self away in taking care of everyone and everything else.
4. Ignoring the needs of self, a feeling that once everyone else is taken care of I'll get around to taking care of myself (which most often does *not* occur).
5. Feeling abandoned, a deep sense of loneliness.

6. Lack of self-worth, a feeling that I'm not good enough.
7. Enormous amounts of guilt most of the time, a personal inner conflict with what my heart desires and what I "should" do.
8. A feeling of being "stuck" for a long period of time.
9. A deep sense of anger and resentment.
10. An overall feeling of resignation and hopelessness.

It is my heart's prayer that this insight will free women everywhere of their inner pain, for it is no longer needed. This message is very clear to me.

I find it interesting that many women who have survived breast cancer ask me if I experience guilt for getting this disease. Again, *I want to stress the importance of not blaming ourselves—for without blame, we cannot experience guilt!* Furthermore, how can we possibly feel guilty if we do not have the awareness or knowledge of how a disease is manifested? I don't believe for a moment that anyone consciously chooses to get sick!

Why are women so drawn to burdening themselves with guilt, particularly after learning that it is one of the commonalities I discovered among women who get breast cancer? Guilt does not acknowledge the needs of our heart as divine. Guilt serves no one. It only creates inner conflict and makes women wrong for wanting to be themselves. If the truth be known, it takes real inner strength to *not* feel guilty. This is, frankly, a new muscle that needs development through conscious awareness. In fact, when we choose to live our lives for ourselves first, I believe we are taking full responsibility for our lives. There is nothing wrong with being less attached to everyone else's needs and taking better care of ourselves. *This teaches others to become more responsible as well, which is valuable!*

The sooner we decide to release these patterns, the quicker and less painful the process will be, and the easier it will be to establish new patterns that truly serve us. In this book I will guide you through this process that I personally have experienced, and continue to experience. My commitment to you is reflective of my commitment to myself. It all begins with honoring ourselves.

My intention is to inspire you to honor your divine feminine spirit, for this is what is tragically lacking among women who get breast cancer. *If we believe that this shift may be nothing short of a formula for AVOIDING breast cancer, then we can change our way of being.* The very fact that you are reading this book demonstrates that you are indeed interested in honoring yourself as a woman. For this, I celebrate with you wholeheartedly.

If you find yourself experiencing fear about

breast cancer at this moment or at any other time, please turn to Chapter 4. Its message offers you a feeling of comfort and peacefulness. It is healthy to acknowledge and accept your feelings as being OK. Allow them to come forth; they deserve to be acknowledged. After you have read Chapter 4, you can return to where you left off. Refer to this chapter as often as you need to.

This book was written to empower you with knowledge that may potentially prevent you from developing breast cancer and other diseases. It is my appreciation for what I have learned that moves me to share with you some of the tools and guidelines for honoring the feminine spirit.

One of the most valuable tools is to ask this question often: "What am I to receive from this?" This is a very powerful question, for the answer, without a doubt, will be a gift to you. This simple question will guide you and teach you to look for the gift in every situation. It is a beautiful way to find light and love, particularly with a situation that seems dark. I personally love this question because it helps me to center myself and to rise above and be bigger than what I initially see as a challenge.

You can take a frustrating situation like being stuck in traffic and choose to hate every minute of it by thinking about what you have to do once you get there. You know you are going to be late, so what do you do? You can choose to tap into your conscious perspective of the feminine spirit and stop yourself from thinking about all the negative possibilities. You can choose to ask yourself, "What am I to receive from this?" More than likely, you will experience yourself breathing again, at the very least!

I remember sitting in traffic once, feeling really upset, and posing this question to myself. As I looked around at the other cars, I noticed a child who was making silly faces directly at me. I immediately started making faces back, and found myself laughing and truly enjoying this little one. The moment I opened myself up to receiving, the gift showed up as a beautiful child who brought me back to a much bigger picture about what really matters. It was important for me to laugh and find joy in that instant. As it turned out, the person I was going to meet was also late, and everything worked out just fine. Now, I view my time in traffic as a gift and am grateful for the time alone.

This tool can also give new meaning to some of the most mundane things we need to do on a daily basis. What is viewed as stressful, or perhaps a hassle, is suddenly viewed with loving eyes. Life flows beautifully as you begin to honor your sacred self. This takes practice, but most of all it takes awareness. I have nothing against To Do lists, as long as they are balanced with your truly being present. You will find that you will get even more done, with more ease, when you tap into this new way of being.

Eliminating thoughts of the "next" frees us up from our mind chatter. It is the mind chatter that usually wears us out, and does not serve us in a way that is healthy. When I speak of mind chatter, I mean the self-talk or "tapes" that our minds play over and over again. It's all about the "shoulds," "coulds," and "woulds." This will be discussed further in Chapter 7, where we will explore our patterns and beliefs.

The way to focus on your divine feminine spirit is to take a deep breath when you find yourself in a stressful situation. Breathe in life, and take a moment to feel your heart, not your pulse! Listen to your inner voice and allow it to guide you. Trust and know that what you hear from within comes from love and from God. This is sacred. Look around you and witness life unfolding in its natural state. Look for the beauty, the power, and the peacefulness of the divine feminine spirit in the eyes of every woman you encounter. It's not about lace and frills. It is a light that is possessed from deep within that brings healing to all who see it. This light is very much in line with what people refer to as the pregnancy glow—the exuberant face of a woman who carries life.

Connect with nature and feel your own power

within it. Receive what is simply waiting to be given to you. Just today, I sat with the trees and fresh scent of spring. Soon I noticed a playful little hummingbird fluttering about, as if to greet me. He settled himself within arm's reach on a tiny twig. I was amazed by how close he sat, and saw comfort in his little blinking eyes. Together we sat for what seemed to be quite some time sharing the wonder of life. Our exchange was one of gratitude for the moment, which filled my heart deeply. Then the phone rang, and we fled to our seemingly separate worlds.

You see, the whole point of receiving is to fill our cup, and respond to a deeper sense of self. Women are vessels. Without receiving, what are we truly giving? When we are full of self-love, we give tirelessly. When we give from nothing, we are constantly fatigued. In addition, our world will mirror and duplicate for us—many times over—either the lack or the abundance of self-love we possess. In other words, if you honor yourself, your world will honor you.

I believe that every woman is being called to a deeper sense of self because our balance is needed in the world today. As humankind evolves, it is evident that we are moving toward a far more spiritual place. We have outgrown the ways of the patriarchs. The partnership of what I refer to as the Divine Dance has already begun. If you look around, you will see that matters of the heart, although painful, are surfacing everywhere in order to heal. Discernment and integrity are being given attention. Men and women are coming together in order to make a real difference in each other's lives. It is simply natural that the awareness of the divine feminine spirit is threading itself throughout all of humanity, for it is this spirit that represents all life forms.

My sense is that our society as a whole has grown tired of the so-called rat race, the millions of things to *do*, and the need to do something at all times. It seems that we are seeking more meaning in life. I believe that the need for spirituality is growing rapidly as a result of our wanting balance in our lives. This is representative of the part of ourselves that is beautifully aligned with the feminine spirit. It is this spirit that is breaking through, much as a baby pushes through its mother's womb during birth. I believe that many of the changes taking place in our society today are directly related to this desire for balance and meaning. Honoring this spirit within us as women allows us to embrace the healing that is occurring among all of humankind and throughout the universe.

Chapter 2   Breast Cancer Is a Symptom

Although many wish to blame the women's movement for a lot of the undesirable changes that have occurred in our society, I feel that this was a vehicle for establishing ourselves as an integral part of society—the beginning stages of a divine partnership. It absolutely had to take place as part of our history.

The women's movement certainly highlighted our rights as women and it has served in creating more choices for us. Choice is an honorable gift.

Many of us have chosen to have careers in addition to establishing our families. Having more choices has led women to believe we can do it all, and many of us do so successfully. However, I believe that the first choice *must* be to honor and take care of the mind, body, and spirit. What has happened to women on a mass level is that most have learned to do it all *without* the balance of the divine feminine spirit.

I wish to establish a new women's movement called the Honor Movement, where women give themselves permission to honor themselves. I believe that breast cancer is merely a symptom of what is occurring for women, and all humankind. In my opinion, breast cancer is just a name given to the enormous dis-ease that women at large are experiencing. According to Julia Rowland, an assistant professor of psychiatry at Georgetown University who specializes in psychological problems of breast cancer, nearly 75 percent of breast cancer cases occur in women with no risk factor, making it seem "to come out of the blue." (Taken from "Emotional Toll Can Be Harsh, But Some Fears Can Be Allayed," by Steve Emmons, *L.A. Times,* October 22, 1995.)

It's true for most women that breast cancer does appear to come out of nowhere. However, I believe there is most definitely a rhyme and reason to its madness. Authorities in both the medical and research fields agree that the occurrence of breast cancer is highest in middle-aged women. At what age do women generally evaluate their self-worth, sense of value, and whether they are honored? This is a most challenging time for most women, for it is a time of many changes. Children have grown up and are moving out of the house; suddenly, less mothering is required. A woman may feel less valuable, and experience the loss of being a full-time mom. In reality, her title has not changed, but her job description has!

At this age a woman may also experience the loss of a parent and the finality that it brings, such as having to sell the house in which she grew up. She may also experience menopause and all of its related physical changes—not to mention the emotional shifts that take place. Clearly, this can be an extremely vulnerable time for any woman. If there was *ever* a time for women to completely immerse themselves in the realm of honoring themselves, this would be it!

I believe that middle-aged women can experience all of these changes with less discomfort if they focus on what makes them feel loved and create a special support system. *It is vital that we give ourselves permission to feel all that we feel WITHOUT making ourselves wrong.* Doing this will give us the strength we need to get through this most tenacious time of cleansing. (I have chosen the word "cleansing" rather than "grieving" because cleansing is a form of metamorphosis.)

Based on all of these changes, it is normal for women to feel vulnerable. It is through vulnerability that we are allowed to experience our highest growth. This is a time that can be used to re-create our lives and start anew. One of the nicest changes that usually happens during this period is the sudden availability of time, especially after children have moved out. However, there can also be a lot of anxiety and restlessness around the uncertainty of what the future holds.

For example, as a mom, perhaps you established traditions for your family that had been passed down to you from prior generations. Suddenly you realize that your children have other plans for the next holiday, and you will be spending it alone with your husband. This is clearly awkward since you're so used to creating a festive dinner and all that goes with it. It seems you've always had a full house. So what do you do? Cooking for two just doesn't feel quite as festive. You think to yourself, "Maybe I should go away with my husband for the weekend."

I've heard it said that the word "crisis" also means "opportunity" in the Chinese language. I believe this is a tremendous opportunity for establishing what you want and opening yourself up to what you can create for yourself, and possibly for your husband. This can be viewed as a new beginning for your relationship.

We need to have compassion for ourselves and for other women—particularly during this time period. It is a lot for one individual to bear alone. Let's face it, any one of these changes can be a great loss in itself. If a woman is experiencing most or all of these changes during her middle years, she may *unconsciously* choose to keep busy so she doesn't have to experience her discomfort. This can lead to much of what I have described within the ten commonalities I found with breast cancer survivors.

It makes perfect sense that a woman who is experiencing all of these changes would want to feel more in control, since her life may feel so *out* of control. Yet these changes are part of our natural cycle, and we can approach them with greater consciousness and understanding.

The key is to be aware of the fact that women are bigger than breast cancer. It may have presented itself in a way that appears to be larger than life, but it is not! Breast cancer simply *cannot* be larger than life, because women represent life!

Many will say that there is a war against breast cancer. In my opinion, we cannot heal breast cancer if we choose to see it as an enemy. A dear friend of mine once said, "You cannot have peace by hating war. You can only have peace by loving peace." If you look around, you'll see that many wars have been established: the war against drunk drivers, AIDS, crime, drugs, cancer, etc. Our entire languaging as a society seems to be one of fighting. *Long live the sword!* appears to be the underlying theme of each ad, program, and campaign for these so-called wars.

When we take a hard look at the issues at hand, we can see that healing is really what we all want. In fact, we need not worry about fighting these wars once we focus on honoring who we are, and acknowledging each other's pain. For example, drunk drivers do not start out their night with the intention of killing anyone. On the contrary, their inner pain is so great that numbing it with alcohol is all they are capable of doing. Those abusing alcohol may or may not be aware of the intensity of their dis-ease. Alcohol simply becomes a vehicle or a way to temporarily ease their discomfort. The alcohol is often seen as the problem, when in fact it is merely a symptom of a deeper problem.

Often the pain is unconsciously ignored, or suppressed. When we unconsciously choose to ignore or suppress our dis-ease, it continues to grow until we finally listen.

I believe it is natural for us to live healthy lives. I don't believe that getting sick is what comes naturally to us. It takes a lot of suppression, and a lot more energy to *not* face a personal sense of dis-ease than it does to simply be with it, experience it, and acknowledge it.

Breast cancer has become so widespread that it has gotten our attention. At times, it appears to be more of a silent killer than heart disease. However, it is not. It is the silence of the dis-ease that I wish to give voice to. *We need not give away our body parts or our lives in order to get the message.* If we pay more attention to what is going on in our hearts, our bodies can live in harmony with our spirit.

Long live the wand! It is the wand that brings in compassion, love, understanding, nurturing, healing, and—ultimately—peace of mind. Place your energy in the wand. Choose to feel these gifts for yourself first and then experience it for others. Becoming aware of any dis-ease or discomfort is the first step in experiencing the power of the wand.

I carry this wand as a flaming torch and it is my privilege to pass it on to you with the same love that it was passed on to me. We can re-create a new world and make this a historical time.

A Lesson in War
by Micki Voisard

When I hear someone use the term "war on cancer" or talk about "battling cancer" my hackles go up.

Maybe it comes from my experience in Vietnam during the war. I was with Flying Tiger Airlines and not directly involved in the fighting but spent plenty of time in the bunkers and also heard endless stories of battles.

In a battle there is a winner and a loser or two losers. Usually even the winner comes out bloodied.

Battles vary in length but usually don't last long.

There is always an enemy and that enemy is portrayed as evil and domineering.

It became evident to me when I was diagnosed with stage 3B ovarian cancer how much war terminology was used to describe the experience a cancer patient was going through.

I listened to that phrase a few times from friends but soon I stopped listening. I don't even want to be referred to as a "cancer survivor." I am not surviving, I'm thriving!

If we put it in terms of finances and you asked me, "How is your financial situation, Micki?"

And I answered you by saying, "It's surviving," what picture comes to your mind of my financial situation?

Turn it around and instead I say, "It's thriving!"

My financial situation can still be shaky but "thriving" gives it a more positive and focused result. But most important, I believe it.

I have found more people who have not had cancer refer to it in war terms, rather than the cancer thrivers themselves.

If someone is "battling" cancer they cannot sustain
    that battle for too long.

As I said earlier, there is always an enemy so I ask you,
    "Who is the enemy if cancer is in your body?"

The "enemy" becomes your own body! How healing is
    that?

Some people have said, "No, the cancer is the enemy."

Go back in history and review actual wars of the past.

As in Vietnam, where we identified the enemy as the
    Vietcong. The entire country, the innocent people,
    and the environment were either killed, maimed,
    or destroyed along with some of the Vietcong.

My point is to stop and consider what we are saying
    and believing. If the quotes "we are what we think"
    and "what we believe we can conceive" are true,
    then you probably get the picture.

Former President Richard Nixon declared the war on
    cancer in the early '70s. It wasn't appropriate
    then and it's not appropriate now.

You don't need to "battle" or "fight" or become a
    "warrior." Tell people, "I'm healing!" Then put

*your energy into enjoying and experiencing your
life. HEAL WITH IT!*

Micki Voisard is a Napa Valley, California, whimsical
wood artist, a speaker on art and healing, and author of *Cancer . . . Then Healing! 16 Decisions to Make
When You or a Loved One Are Told "You Have Cancer."*

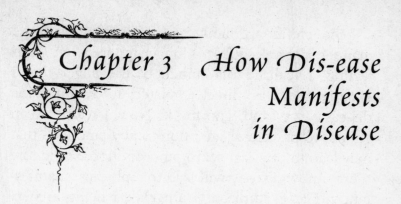

Chapter 3 How Dis-ease Manifests in Disease

When I speak of dis-ease, I am referring to the specific discomfort that occurs within the heart. It initiates in the mind as a thought which is followed by an emotion. It then transfers itself into the body as a physical reaction or response. For example, when you hear news that is disturbing, you may experience anger, which increases your heart rate and your blood pressure. Your body responds directly to what you are feeling and thinking. The intensity of the physical manifestation is a clear result of the intensity of the emotion.

At times, dis-ease appears as "something that just doesn't feel right," sort of a gut feeling. It can be a subtle yet deep feeling of not being truly understood, heard, or respected. Because of its subtlety, it is easy to miss or ignore. However, it is important to recognize that once it is ignored, it can and most likely will show itself in a way that guarantees your attention.

The cancer certainly got my attention in a manner where I could no longer ignore what I was feeling. I realized that much of the anger that I experienced was directly related to wishing the dis-ease away and ignoring it. Now, I realize I can choose to pay closer attention to any emotions that may lead to physical symptoms, or choose to ignore them, knowing they will lead to a physical manifestation. For example, if I am experiencing anxiety and choose to wish it away, I may experience a severe headache. I can then choose to either take something to relieve the pain or sit with the anxiety and understand its origin. This is how powerful both the heart and the mind are.

Our emotions are much like children. For example, when a child calls "mommy" more than once without being acknowledged by the mother, he/she may continue to carry on to the point of a tantrum. Once the mother focuses all of her attention on the child by holding and loving him/her, the child is quiet. All the screaming and demanding goes away.

So when I choose to sit with my emotions, I am choosing to accept them for what they are. I can sit in meditation, or with my journal, and allow myself to feel the emotion and its intensity. I can get to the root of it so it won't haunt me again. I can love it like a friend instead of experiencing it as an enemy.

Understanding how the heart and the mind work brings aliveness to the spirit. Without clarity we fall victim to suffering, both emotionally and physically. A good example of this is the woman who wishes to talk with her husband when he comes home from work. As it turns out, he's exhausted from his day and is sitting in front of the television set looking for something to watch. She begins to talk about some things that are important to her. Her partner, on the other hand, unconsciously tunes her out. Yet she continues to talk, hoping for some attention and acknowledgment. He nods occasionally, completely unaware of what she's talking about!

She feels a bit of dis-ease, sensing that he's not listening. So why do you think she keeps talking? She continues for two reasons:

1. She doesn't want to believe that her husband doesn't care, and
2. She's hoping that out of the million topics she's touched on, something, *anything*, will get his attention!

It's painful, because she'll eventually just wear herself out and feel empty inside, never having achieved a *real* conversation. It seems that the less she gets, the more she gives. She grows silent within her frustration and buries her emotions. Her mind chatter steps in. She finds herself physically exhausted and helpless.

What started out as a simple conversation grew

into a desperate cry for attention. The instant she noticed that her husband wasn't being attentive was the moment she began to ignore her own feelings by continuing to talk. As many women do, she unconsciously began to feel unimportant. Furthermore, a pattern established itself, as this scenario reoccurred time and time again. This created a tremendous drain on her sense of confidence, self-esteem, and ability to communicate with others. Not feeling loved by her mate outside her bedroom caused her to feel unloved by her world. Feeling unloved led to overmothering because mothering was all that was left! It was too painful otherwise, so she kept busy *doing* for others and detached herself from her inner core feelings.

It seemed that the bigger the void she felt within, the more she gave, and the more she continued to feel unworthy—until her body began to break down. It's no wonder that, in many cases, women who are diagnosed with breast cancer are simultaneously divorcing their husbands.

This woman was me, and I am grateful to say I did *not* have to divorce my husband as a result of this dis-ease. This was a pattern that I unconsciously established early on in my marriage and I suffered immensely because of it. It affected every aspect of my life, as it directly created a lack of self-worth and contributed to the erosion of my self-esteem. I felt and experienced many of the ten commonalities, including anger, resentment, abandonment, guilt, ignoring of self, hopelessness, and overmothering. This is just one example of the various forms this dis-ease can take.

To make matters worse, I translated and reaffirmed each frustrating conversation with my own negative self-talk. This only compounded other issues I was already dealing with, such as being a first-time mom and choosing to stay home. While changing diapers and doing the laundry, I would find myself longing for some form of recognition. I knew I had made the right choice in staying home to raise my son, but I deeply missed the business world. I missed the simplest things—like being with people, having stimulating conversations, dressing professionally, and most of all making a difference in people's lives.

At times my heart felt torn in half, as I treasured special moments with my son, not wanting to miss any of them. I desperately wanted to be completely happy like other moms, yet I craved going back to work. When I did leave for a work appointment, guilt would strike as I left with my child crying for me. How many of us have cried when we've left our babies? On the other hand, it was exhilarating to get up, shower, and know that one of my clients was looking forward to seeing me.

I had mastered hiding my inner pain, not only

from others, but also from myself, by keeping very busy. I would go out of my way to please others regardless of how exhausted I was, because I felt better about myself (temporarily).

In my lack of awareness, I blamed my husband John for much of my unhappiness. My anger toward myself showed up as depression, which was difficult to deny. Again, it is important to mention that I don't blame myself, because I was completely unaware of what was occurring. Understanding these patterns allowed me to stop blaming John. It gave me a reason to take full responsibility for my own happiness and consciously choose a different way of being.

Unfortunately, a dis-ease can magnify itself to the point that it manifests itself in a disease, much as it did in my case. This is why I am so passionate and driven to share what I've learned! I know in my heart (as do many survivors) that if I had allowed myself the same level of authentic self-expression that I integrated into my life *after* my diagnosis, there would have *been* no diagnosis. It's all simply a matter of awareness.

(So, if you ever find yourself in a conversation where the person you're speaking with is not truly present with you, you owe it to yourself and that person to stop. Ask him or her to tell you when would be a better time to talk. Give him or her an opportunity to participate in this conversation that's important to you. You might also choose to write your feelings down in the form of a letter. Most important, communicate how you feel *without making assumptions about how the other person feels about you.*)

In short, dis-ease is your inner voice letting you know that something isn't sitting well with you. I look at it as a red flag and have learned to use it as a guideline for what needs to be addressed in my life. I have found it to be exceptionally rewarding to pay attention to these red flags. There is so much to learn about oneself by just stopping and feeling.

There are times when it is tempting to ignore those red flags, particularly when we are excited about our work and having a great time. When I started my career as one of the first personal shoppers at Nordstrom in South Coast Plaza, California, it was one of the most exciting times of my life. This was considered a pioneer store since it was the first store built outside of its home state of Washington. I remember sitting in a meeting with the store manager and other managers and buyers; the main thrust of the meeting was to inspire us to go out and make Nordstrom a household name. At the time, the Nordstroms believed in using only word-of-mouth referrals for advertising. Part of my job was to introduce Nordstrom to various groups and organizations and speak about wardrobe coordination and the service we provided. I carried with me a wardrobe of fifteen to twenty pieces of merchandise and demonstrated how to coordinate them into various outfits. I felt so valued as an employee, Nordstrom soon became "my life." It was a joy having people who had never heard of Nordstrom literally get into their car and follow me back to the store! Not only was the merchandise easy to sell, it was tremendously rewarding to provide the best service ever known to customers in the fashion industry.

My incredible enthusiasm and love for the company led me to work many long hours and many days in a row. In the five years that I worked for Nordstrom, I gave more than five hundred talks and workshops, addressing the growing needs of women and men in the area of image and fashion. The experience I gained during this time is invaluable and cannot be described. Nordstrom will always have a special place in my heart.

Yet, during those five years I began to experience fatigue and problems with my health. Looking back, this was a red flag that I unconsciously ignored. I believe that I was so busy being excited I simply did not take proper care of myself. Given the opportunity to do it all again, I would gladly do so, except this time I would listen to my body, eat three meals a day, and rest when I needed to.

I experienced a lot of dis-ease while I was learning to be assertive and businesslike. I learned what was appropriate and what was not by watching other women. All of my time was spent in the male energy of *doing*. I became my work, and my work became me. As long as I was working, I was in my comfort zone.

Ironically, walking into a room full of women was extremely uncomfortable, particularly a bridal or baby shower. Sadly, my view of these women at the time was that they were immature. The games they played at these functions seemed senseless and purposeless. I simply couldn't relate, and I'd find myself completely bored! On the outside, I appeared to be as feminine as any woman. On the inside, I had trained myself to carry the sword! I became rather attached to my sword. And I placed a Band-Aid on my dis-ease by viewing other women as being silly or less than perfect.

After leaving Nordstrom, I ventured into starting my own business as a wardrobe consultant. My true sense of satisfaction was derived from becoming extremely confident in my work, which I enjoyed immensely. My greatest reward was witnessing the personal growth and blossoming self-confidence of the individuals I worked with. My greatest joy was watching someone come alive and feel "like a million dollars." I felt so in control of my life, and so powerful!

The real shock came when I got married and started having children. There was no room for the control I had grown so attached to. Furthermore, to me the term "housewife" was demeaning and inappropriate. I hadn't married a house!

During this time, I found it refreshing to help my husband with his professional activities. Helping him create his business plan and set goals, and accompanying him to various conventions where he was acknowledged for his accomplishments, was very rewarding. Even though I wasn't being acknowledged directly, it was exciting to share in his triumphs. It was a high for me because I missed the challenges of the business world.

In that world, wielding the sword in the male spirit was second nature. However, there was no place for the sword in my daily routine as a mother and wife! Looking back, I can clearly see times when I unconsciously created difficult situations in my life that allowed me to bring out that sword! Some of these situations showed up as power struggles with John. I would bring out the sword to fight for issues I felt I was right about, just to prove my self-worth to myself and to him.

Some say that it takes five years for cancer to make itself known. I was two months short of my fifth wedding anniversary with John when I learned about my breast cancer. Fortunately, my marriage with John was and continues to be quite strong. I believe that the inner conflict I struggled with, along with immense guilt and the need for control, were signs that something had to change in my life. I needed to find value in myself and in my life again.

In the mid-1980s, I had the honor of meeting Louise L. Hay, the brilliant and inspiring author of *Heal Your Body*. In person, she is every bit as magnificent as her books and teachings. In *Heal Your Body*, she speaks not only of her own encounter with cancer, but also of her healing journey, which involved the mental process of releasing and forgiving. She goes on to link specific physical problems with probable emotional causes, and then offers a new thought pattern as a positive healing affirmation.

I have found her healing affirmations to be very enlightening, and a special gift to all who seek personal expansion. How truly wonderful it is to understand what the dis-ease or physical ailment is trying to tell us. Once we can recognize the emotions and messages underlying the dis-ease, we can begin to change the thought and behavioral patterns that could lead to manifestation of a disease. The healing of a disease begins where the dis-ease began: in the heart and in the mind.

Chapter 4   *Fear Does Not Exist in the Present*

Needless to say, "fear" seems to be breast cancer's middle name. It's no wonder that the two appear to go hand in hand, based on what most women equate breast cancer with: everything from losing one's breast to losing one's life. This fear is normal and significant.

When we take a closer look, however, we can begin to see that fear does not reside in the moment. *At this very moment you are safe,* and you are very much alive! Fear lives only in the past and in the future—*not* in the present. Release and free yourself of any concerns, for they don't pertain to this moment in time. Simply clear your mind of any "what-if's." Feel the relief as you let go of them, and focus your energy on what you are experiencing in this moment as you are reading.

Fear of breast cancer serves no one. It is simply another form of dis-ease—one that needs to be addressed so we don't give it our power. Our energy flows where our attention goes. I find it valuable to do a reality check on fear from time to time.

I'll share a story with you about fear that I found most interesting. Shortly after my son Christopher started his second season of T-ball, I met a mother who openly shared her feelings of fear about the game. She said she hated the game because she was afraid her son would get hit in the head with the ball. And if I hadn't been there to witness it, I would never have believed it: I don't think there was a game when her little boy didn't get hit with the ball! Fortunately, it never resulted in a severe injury, but it was unbelievable! This woman's fear grew stronger with every game. Every time her son got hit, the power of her fear magnified as she believed she was right.

I feel that this is what happens when we (unconsciously) pay more attention to the fear of what we *don't* want, rather than focusing on what we *do* want. Fear is sometimes strange in the sense that we can literally bring to us what we fear the most. Because we create energy with our thoughts and beliefs, it's a good idea to evaluate and check in with our fear(s).

Fear can seem real, without being based on reality. One way to evaluate whether our fear is serving us is to look at whether there is real danger or simply an example of what the mind is capable of creating.

✦ If the danger is real, then our fear is
   actually a form of wisdom. In this case,
   our fear serves to protect us.

✦ Counterproductive fear can derive from a
   lack of trust or too much focus on what
   we don't want to have happen in our lives.
   This fear does not serve or protect us.

Although fear can wear many different disguises,
here's a way to decide whether it is wisdom or just a
possibility. The next time you are confronted with
fear, ask yourself: "Is this fear preventing me from
real danger, or is it springing from a negative possibility that my mind has created?"

For example, I do not allow my children to ride
in the car without seat belts. In my opinion, not using seat belts places my children in real danger.
Thus, this fear is actually wisdom, and it is appropriate. When I stay focused on their safety and
make sure they're wearing seat belts, the fear goes
away and does not haunt me.

On the other hand, I can choose to experience
fear about the possibility of breast cancer reoccurring. This fear does not protect me from real danger.
It serves only to place energy into something I *don't*
want, and something that is *not* real. Although the
fear may *feel* very real and present, it is a result of
what my mind has created. Knowing I have a clean

bill of health and staying focused on honoring myself eliminates the haunting "what-if's."

Examine and identify your fear and decide whether it serves you or not.

- ✦ When fear serves you, there is a tendency to feel a sense of comfort and peace when it is addressed, as with my example of the seat belts.
- ✦ When fear does not serve you, it can haunt you intensely from time to time. Addressing this type of fear may feel overwhelming, and even more frightening than what you're feeling fear about.

Understanding this distinction allows us to recognize when fear is a vital part of our self-protection, and guides us to consciously choose where we place our energy.

As another example, many women flatly refuse to do a breast self-examination for *fear* that they might "find something." This fear is not protecting them from real danger. It is a fear the mind has created based on the possibilities of the unknown. If anything, it will only become stronger, along with the resistance. In this case, fear immobilizes the individual and becomes bigger than the reality. In this example, succumbing to the fear itself is far more dangerous than the imagined possibility. In fact, the possibility is fed by the fear itself, giving it power and providing us with Murphy's Law. I believe we place ourself at higher risk when we choose to deny ourselves important knowledge versus taking an active part in learning as much as we can about our bodies. In addition, more energy will be spent on the fear than would be needed by taking a few minutes to do a breast self-exam. *It is far more exhausting to live in fear!*

During my healing, I met a woman who had chosen to have a bilateral mastectomy, which is a surgical procedure where breast tissue is completely removed from both breasts. This woman was healthy and had not been diagnosed with breast cancer. It was her intense fear that led her to make this choice. Due to the fact that other women in her family had been diagnosed, she simply felt it was just a matter of time before she, too, would discover a lump. Although I place absolutely no judgment on her, I do feel for her. Unfortunately, her results were reflective of her fear, and she suffered tremendously. Her need to eliminate the fear created a sense of urgency for the procedure. This was reflected in the energy of the doctors, and many things went wrong during and after the surgery. I was sad to hear that she felt disfigured and that her implants, along with her reconstruction, were not as successful as she would have liked. The irony for me was that we had both worked with the same two surgeons, who are known for their high level of skill, expertise, and success; and my results were very successful.

When we fear, we open ourselves up to all kinds of possibilities that stand in the way of our inner guidance. Our minds become clouded with awful scenarios and our angels who are there to guide us cannot do their work. There is a beautiful book called *Angel Blessings* by Kimberly Marooney, complete with cards of sacred guidance and inspiration. It describes forty-four angels and what each represents in divine love. I refer to this book on a daily basis, and have found it to be truly wonderful. From one of the eight "spreads" (card arrangements) available for inner growth and transformation, I select three cards at random. This particular spread is called "attunement," which aligns my body, mind, and soul with the angels. It is very powerful to know which angels are choosing to align with me. The accuracy of the information I receive never ceases to amaze me.

For example, the three cards I just pulled as part of my inspiration for this chapter are Ramaela (the angel of joy), Remiel (the angel of mercy), and Zacharael (the angel of surrender). I couldn't have chosen three better angels to guide us through fear.

Focusing our attention on these angels may help alleviate our fears and elevate our spirit. There is much comfort in knowing we are loved and divinely guided. I'd like to share a bit of what Kim Marooney has written for each of these very special angels.

Ramaela (the angel of joy)—"There is joy in the presence of angels." [Luke 15:10] Do you welcome opportunities for joy? Knowledge, truth, vision, and life are also expressions of joy. This daily state of awareness has to do with your attitude as you concentrate on work, home, and family. Has your life become drudgery? Do you complain? Does it bring you energy? Are you excited or bored? Joyfulness is energizing and creative, *automatically attuning you with angels.* When you follow the feelings that make you joyful, your joyline, you accept the guidance of your eternal self and your spiritual destiny. If circumstances aren't as you wish, use your imagination and ask for Ramaela to transform boredom into playful creativity.

Remiel (the angel of mercy)—Remiel means "the mercy of God." Mercy is justice tempered by wisdom, which grows out of knowledge and understanding. Divine mercy represents a technique of adjustment between perfection and imperfection, of fairness, and is one of the basic concepts of Creation. Since God knows everything about each of us, it is easy for Divine Spirit to forgive. "God's mercy endures forever."

Zacharael (the angel of surrender)—Zacharael means "the remembrance of God." When you surrender, you are remembering that you are a fragment of God. Deep surrender opens the connection with your eternal self, which is your personalized manifestation of an important aspect of God. The greatest illusion we face is that we are the small self of everyday life. We get trapped into believing that we are the emotional baggage and images assembled from past experiences. Be willing to surrender the ego and its collection of small-minded, critical, negative beliefs that separate you from others and from the love of God. The thought of surrender is frightening at first. If you have no experience with this, you can only relate it to a feeling of helplessness and vulnerability. When there has been no personal experience of the presence of God, or recognizable answers to prayer, the concept of surrender seems dangerous. The power of faith acts to help you leap into the unknown. Your faith in the angels, a power greater than yourself, the ultimate truth, Jesus, or whatever is meaningful to you, provides the bridge. Gradually, one experience at a time, you begin to feel God, your eternal self, or the angels in a personal way. You recognize their presence and receive answers to prayers. Your trust grows as you learn to communicate and feel their power.

There is no place for fear when we choose to embrace the message these angels have presented here. When we have joy in our hearts, when we are merciful and forgiving with ourselves and others, and when we choose to surrender our fear, we are choosing to transform. It is our willingness to transform that disarms our fear. Peacefulness revisits us as we acknowledge our inner power.

I believe that fear is also learned. For example, we have been told that breast cancer is "an epidemic." The term "epidemic" means the spread of a contagious disease. Clearly, there has been no proof to support the wide use of this term in relation to breast cancer. It is a word that does nothing except create enormous fear in women. It creates an energy that is not healthy for us. This is an example of a counterproductive, fear-based statement.

We need not be afraid of breast cancer if we choose to play an active role in knowing our bodies by doing monthly breast self-exams, getting regular check-ups, and following up with a mammogram/

ultrasound. Early detection is the key and can save your life. Having made it to the other side, I can tell you that *early detection is what saved my life.*

Something that I find most helpful in dealing with fear is to communicate to a loved one what you are experiencing. This might be a husband or a dear friend. Choose someone you can trust to kindly listen to your concerns. In my experience, it made all the difference in the world to involve my husband every step of the way. I experienced a great sense of comfort when I communicated my fears to him.

I'd like to share a bit of my personal story and what I learned about fear so you may view this disease with fresh eyes. Breast cancer does not have to mean disfiguration, nor does it have to mean death.

John and I were on a business trip when I first discovered a lump the size of a small grape under my left arm. Because I didn't know that women in their thirties could get breast cancer, that thought never entered my mind. I also didn't know that the region just below the armpit is considered breast tissue. I find it somewhat miraculous that I found it while lying on my side.

As soon as I found it, I turned to John and asked him to tell me what he thought. In a matter-of-fact tone of voice, he encouraged me to have it checked out. During the seven days of our trip, I noticed that the lump could only be felt while lying on my side.

I looked for it every time I showered, but it was no-where to be found.

Although I didn't experience fear, I *was* anxious to find out what it was. Since my primary physician was not available, I chose to see the first available doctor on staff. I will always hold a special place in my heart for Dr. Richard Kammerman, who sent me for a mammogram. My experience with the mam-mogram was an interesting one, since it showed no sign of cancer. It was the persistence and expertise of the technician and the doctor at the facility that led me to have an ultrasound, which ultimately re-vealed the mass. I am deeply grateful to these two individuals for checking further, after viewing two sets of films that showed no sign of anything serious nor reason for concern! They could easily have let me walk out the door thinking I was just fine.

I later learned that the ultrasound differentiates a mass as being solid or fluid-filled. The reason the cancer did not show up on the mammogram is that women who are younger than thirty-five years old tend to have breast tissue that is dense versus fat. The density makes it difficult to detect a mass. As a layper-son I could see the mass on the ultrasound screen as a solid black, perfectly shaped circle. Although my anxiety began to grow, I still didn't think it could be cancer. With the exception of one aunt on my father's side, no one in my family had had breast cancer.

Dr. Kammerman called and kindly referred me to Dr. John West, a surgeon at the Breast Care Center in the city of Orange. Prior to my experience, I had no idea that there was a place such as this where all of my needs could be attended to. The staff included surgeons, oncologists, and women who volunteered their time solely for the purpose of supporting other women. I might add that most of the volunteers were breast cancer survivors, which was comforting.

When I met Dr. West, I sensed right away that he was an energetic, happy, and confident person. He acknowledged John as well as me, which was very important. After looking at my record, he took another ultrasound to confirm the findings. Within minutes he concluded that I needed a biopsy. He explained that he could do a needle biopsy or he could remove the small lump completely. I immediately opted to have the lump surgically removed.

Dr. West assured us that, given its size, it probably wasn't anything serious. He also explained that his specialty was breast surgery and that the procedure would be a very simple one. He showed me the location and size of the incision he would make, which put me right at ease. And he told us that the pathologist would most likely be able to give us the results by the time I woke up from surgery.

I was so relieved to know that this mystery

would be resolved in just a couple of days. Both John and I were very impressed with Dr. West and the time he took to explain everything.

My first and most significant confrontation with fear came when I awoke after surgery. Dr. West told us that the lump had been removed, and the pathologist had said it had some characteristics that were suspicious. Dr. West reassured us that even if it was cancer, it had been caught very early. However, we wouldn't know until the next day.

Well, within the next twenty-four hours, I started to feel that it wasn't cancer that would kill me, but the enormous fear of the unknown. As I held my ten-month-old daughter, Arianna, and my four-year-old son, Christopher, I began to experience all kinds of "what-if's." I woke up in the middle of the night sobbing with John, as the fear of the terrible possibilities jolted us both. We held each other and he told me he couldn't bear the thought of life without me. I will never forget how strong the fear was that night.

Ironically, when the call came from Dr. West telling me it was cancer, I felt amazingly strong. He said that the affected tissue was very small and the margins were clean, meaning that he felt they got it all.

Experiencing the rawness of the intense fear the night before somehow gave me enormous strength.

I immediately began to envision the next ten, twenty, thirty, forty, and fifty years of my life with my husband and my family. In my mind, I saw my children getting married and having children of their own. It was as if a bell went off in my head, and nothing was going to stop me from really living life! As I waited for my husband to pick me up so we could drive to the doctor's office, I began to list questions on paper that I knew would lead me to heal. I knew what I needed to do. I felt so filled with life that two days later John and I took the children to Disneyland!

I learned a great deal from fear that night. I learned that by embracing it completely, it empowered me throughout my entire healing process. Though the fear itself was very real, what I feared the most was not a real threat. Oddly enough, *my fear of losing my life gave me my life back!* What an extraordinary gift!

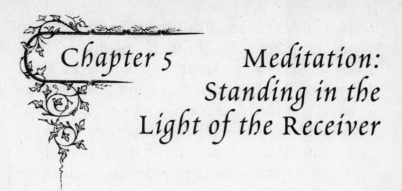

Chapter 5   Meditation: Standing in the Light of the Receiver

Listening to your heart, finding out who you are is not simple. It takes time for the chatter to quiet down. In the silence of "not doing" we begin to know what we feel. If we listen and hear what is being offered, then anything in life can be our guide. Listen.

—SUE BENDER

I believe that in order to fully grasp the concept of meditation, one must understand the meaning of spiritualism. Spiritualism is the relationship with self that mirrors the love of God. It is the deepest form of relationship that we can have. It is unconditional, pure, and perfect. It is universal, for when you are spiritual, you are one with the entire universe. It is a language that is spoken without words. It graces your being with an overwhelming feeling of love and well-being, known to some as euphoria.

Meditation is a beautiful retreat away from the hustle and bustle of everyday life, and it grounds us in spirituality. It is said that twenty minutes of deep meditation is equivalent to six hours of sleep. This is why it is so beneficial to those who practice it as a daily ritual. It has a way of helping us to not feel pulled in so many directions. Without a doubt, taking a break from all our self-talk enables us to feel more centered and realigned with our own truth.

There are many forms of meditation. Some people refer to meditation as a time of reflection or contemplation. In this chapter I am referring to deep meditation: the sacred space of timelessness, silence, and serenity.

In prayer, we speak, we give, or put out thought. In meditation, we listen, we receive, and we take in thought. Although they both come from the same source, they are quite distinctive in purpose.

The messages that we receive within the silence of meditation are invaluable. Inspiration and creativity often sprout in this space of stillness. It is not mere coincidence that what our heart desires begins to manifest in our life, much like small miracles.

My entire process of healing from breast cancer was, without a doubt, not only magical but also quite miraculous. Seven months prior to my diagnosis I was drawn to the audiocassette companion to Shirley MacLaine's bestseller *Going Within*. I purchased it as soon as I saw it, instinctively knowing that I needed to listen to it. I had heard of her wonderful work but had never experienced it firsthand. This was my introduction to meditation, a very powerful one at that!

Shirley offers two extraordinary meditations, as explained on the back cover of Shirley MacLaine's audiocassette, *Going Within; Meditations for Relaxation and Stress Reduction*. The first teaches you about the chakras, which are seven centers of energy that run vertically along your spine and correspond to seven emotional issues of your personality. It is through visualizing the healing light of the chakras that the body, mind, and spirit can be aligned and emotional issues resolved. The second meditation is a beautiful one that helped me focus on aligning myself in my relationships with people.

I listened to this tape every day religiously for seven months. I know in my heart that the tape was a true blessing in disguise. I found myself completely aligned and full of inner power at the time of my diagnosis. In fact, many thought I was in denial as a result of how centered I was.

I continued to use these meditations throughout my entire healing process, as they became a significant part of me. I also chose to wear earphones with the tape playing while I was unconscious during my surgeries. This was to avoid anything less than positive to enter my consciousness, a suggestion that Dr. Bernie Siegel makes in his book *Peace, Love and Healing*.

I found meditation to be my best friend. Throughout my journey it continued to inspire me to not only envision but to *create* exactly how I wanted to heal. It is clear that we can *absolutely* create on the outside what we visualize in our mind through meditation. My extraordinary results offer proof, for I am healed.

There is a special meditation I call "Standing in the Light of the Receiver." I wish to share it with you, for it is a gift to all women. I encourage you to use it on a daily basis. It will expand your awareness and help you discover the gifts in your life.

(Note: You may choose to read through this meditation first and then allow yourself to do the process, or you may have someone read it to you slowly, in a soft and soothing voice. Be sure to pause and allow enough time for the visualization to occur.)

STANDING IN THE LIGHT OF THE RECEIVER

Begin by choosing a quiet place where you can sit in a comfortable position—ideally, with your feet touching the earth. Rest your hands on your lap with your palms open, facing upward.

Relax your body and take in a slow, long breath. Exhale very slowly, intentionally releasing any tension you might feel in your body. Now close your eyes and focus your attention on the middle of your forehead. Take another deep, slow breath, and relax your mind.

Picture yourself standing with your arms opened

and extended, as if you are preparing to embrace someone. Now visualize a white light coming in from the top
of your crown chakra [the top of your head] and
slowly cascading into every cell of your body. You can
see it as a slow-moving waterfall gently flowing into
your face, neck, chest, shoulders, into your arms and
hands, and out through your fingertips.

Feel the warmth and love this light brings as it continues to flow into your torso, hips, thighs, knees, ankles,
and down through your toes and heels into the earth.
See yourself as a radiant body of light. Feel yourself being one with the Infinite Creator, your God. Know that
you are deeply loved, for you are God's child.

Now, visualize what you wish to receive in your life.
Take a moment and receive in your arms what you truly
wish to receive on a personal level [pause], on a physical level [pause], on an emotional level [pause], and on
a financial level [pause].

Receive these gifts, for they come from love. Know
with all your heart that you were meant to receive abundance. Feel every cell of your body receive what you desire. As you embrace these gifts, know that they are a
part of you. You are filled with tremendous gratitude.
The white light bathes you, and you feel sacred.

Now take a moment and take a deep breath. Breathe
in the light, and know that you can bring in this light
any time, for it lives within you. Know that what you visualize, you can create in your world, for you are in direct line with the Infinite Creator [pause].

When you're ready, gently come back to your surroundings and open your eyes.

I feel it is important to log what you saw yourself receiving as soon as you have completed the meditation. It's fascinating to keep a record of what manifests in your life as a result of this process.

This is called a "guided meditation" because you are being gently guided as you visualize. I feel it is easier for the individual who has never meditated to use this process as a starting point. *Remember to not judge your process: It is not about DOING, it's about BEING.* In the beginning, working with a guided meditation is a lot easier than just sitting completely still and quieting the mind. It took me a while before I could just shut off the chatter and *be*— without judging! The more I began to trust, the less I judged myself and the more I learned about being.

Take time to find what is comfortable for you. Experiment with background music, perhaps an instrumental—something that gives you a sense of serenity.

It is ideal if you can meditate for thirty minutes in the morning and in the evening. I believe that the ultimate goal is to replace the space where mind chatter once lived with the silence found in the stillness. When you love inner silence, you love thyself.

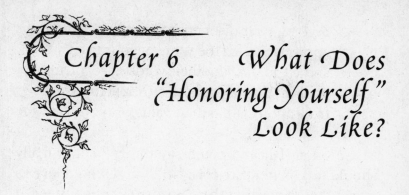

Chapter 6 — What Does "Honoring Yourself" Look Like?

When we think of the word "honor," many of us have an idea of what it means but don't know how to apply it in everyday life. Let's take a look at its meaning so we can begin to integrate it and own it as part of who we are.

What does the word "honor" mean to you? What comes to mind when you think of this word? Although there are many ways to describe it, *American Heritage Dictionary* clearly defines it with four beautiful words: esteem, respect, glory, and distinction. So, when I speak of honoring yourself I am speaking of:

+ Holding yourself in high esteem, and acknowledging your own self-worth.
+ Having a great deal of respect for yourself and your needs.
+ Finding glory in who you are and what you stand for. Singing your own praises!

✦ Seeking your distinction through
appreciation for the value of your talents
and attributes. In other words, recognizing
your unique talents and attributes and
truly appreciating their value.

So often, I hear women say things like, "I really should take better care of myself," or "I would love to go see that movie, but there just isn't enough time." It seems that what the heart wants is usually acknowledged. Yet, honor is given away to other things or people that are considered more important.

My point is that when a woman continually falls short of getting what she wants, it is natural for her to complain. She continues with her life, hoping to get what she wants in the future. Each time this happens, she gives away a part of her self, and after a while this deprivation is reflected in her mood and potentially her physical health.

The following sentences are based on my own experience of honoring myself on a daily basis. They are presented to help you reinforce some of the areas in your life where you can honor yourself.

✦ I know I'm a happier mom when I take
the time for me.
✦ I can come back to my work with fresh
eyes when I allow myself time to rest.

+ When I meditate I feel grounded and not pulled in so many directions.
+ I am a happier person when I allow myself to say "no" to any further commitments.

My suggestion to all women is to step into the space of honoring yourself today. It's the little things you can do for yourself that make the biggest difference. You need not look to the future for what you can do today. When you wake up in the morning, you can choose to say to yourself, "I honor myself."

Although there are many variations of what each unique individual needs in order to feel honored, the outcome is the same. Ultimately, the feeling of being honored creates a sense of well-being, love, and satisfaction with our lives.

In summary, I have created ten steps as a guideline to help you with your process of honoring yourself. They are based on some of the information I have shared with you thus far. I call them "A Woman's Ten Sacred Steps to Living a Balanced Life." They are very special to me, for they keep me aligned with my inner self. With a little practice, I have consciously made them a part of me and my life. These are also celebrations of beautiful patterns that have replaced old patterns.

A Woman's Ten Sacred Steps to Living a Balanced Life

Step 1: Take fifteen to twenty minutes a day to sit alone in silence. Choose a place and time where you will have no distractions. At first, you may want to include this in your list of things to do, as a reminder. With practice it will become second nature and you will look forward to it every day. During this time, you can choose to meditate and quiet the mind.

Step 2: Listen to your inner voice and trust whatever comes your way. Your instincts feed this inner voice and come from love, unlike the mind chatter, which is poison for your mind, body, and spirit. Allow your instincts to guide you, for they are usually correct and right for you.

Step 3: If you haven't already, get acquainted with your personal needs and desires. See yourself receive what you long for and deserve. For example, one of your needs may be receiving more attention from the man in your life—perhaps by getting flowers from him or being taken out to dinner somewhere special for no apparent reason. Seeing it in your mind's eye automatically puts it in the realm of possibility.

Step 4: Communicate your needs to your loved ones. Be clear in stating your truth. If you come from a place of respecting your own needs, you will be amazed at how much you will be respected. Your loved ones want to be part of your happiness, and this is a great way to include them. It empowers them to participate. Remember to use "I" statements as an ownership of your feelings. Remember not to decide in advance what they will say. Let their inner beauty shine by honoring your wishes. Let them know that they are making a difference in your life.

Step 5: Watch your self-talk and replace any message that does not serve you with an empowering affirmation. Remember, you create what you believe in your life, and you can re-create your life with new beliefs.

Step 6: Choose to live in the moment regardless of what's happening, especially during stressful times. Whatever the situation, stop and ask yourself, "What am I to receive from this? What can I learn from this?" Look for the gifts. Experience miracles as you live in the moment.

Step 7: Give yourself permission to take time for whatever is important to you. It might be sitting in a luxurious aromatic bath or reading a great book. If you're like most women, you have given the gift of time to many people and situations. Now give yourself permission to enjoy your time, regardless of how you choose to spend it. If you need to schedule it, then do so, as you would with other weekly appointments.

Step 8: Know your body and your monthly cycle.

Listen to your body, for it is a sacred temple. Pamper yourself during the days of menstruation. Know that this is not a "curse" but a sacred time. It is natural for you to not feel like doing much and to feel sensitive at this time. Allow yourself to feel what is natural.

Step 9: Be gentle with your body. Bless and nurture it with fresh and healthy foods. Find a form of exercise that is enjoyable and not stressful. Walking and bicycling are gentle ways of feeling invigorated with little effort.

Step 10: Choose to do a monthly breast self-examination. In Chapter 13, I will show you the simple steps for doing this. For women who are menstruating, it is important to do this three to five days after your menses. Women who no longer have menses can choose the same day of every month. In either case, you can mark the day you choose in your calendar as a day for pampering. For example, you might choose to have your hair or nails done on this day. The idea is to treat yourself and relax. This day should not be filled with a million appointments. You will find yourself in a positive state of mind and it will be easier to concentrate on the breast exam. Knowing your body eliminates fear. Taking responsibility for your breast health can be effortless and very rewarding.

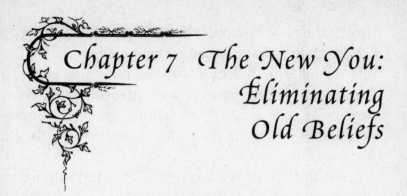

Chapter 7 The New You: Eliminating Old Beliefs

As you become aligned with the divine feminine spirit, it is imperative that you evaluate which of your beliefs truly serve you. For example, many of us carry beliefs that were passed down from earlier generations, and were never ours to begin with. Still, we unconsciously or consciously believe that they are our own.

Because times have changed since these past generations, it seems logical that it would be appropriate for us to shed some of our outdated beliefs. For example, in my mother's generation it was believed that "the doctor knows best." (For the record, I have an enormous respect for doctors and the work they do.) In times past, a woman believed that her doctor knew more about her body than she did, because *she was never taught to know her body*.

As a result, very few questions were asked of doctors, and second opinions were not the norm. Many women accepted the cards they were dealt as "fate," and unconsciously gave away their power. Unfortunately, many became victims when they fell into the hands of a doctor who did not know better. There are countless cases of women who signed papers prior to a surgical procedure, giving doctors permission to remove their uterus or a breast if they felt it was necessary.

It is the cry of the women who needlessly lost their body parts, and those who lose their lives, that I speak for. Their stories are deeply heartfelt. I am moved by many who have come forth to share their stories for the very first time. For these women, the emotional trauma is as vivid today as it was decades ago. It is their suffering that has led to change in the way things can be and are being done today, particularly in what we believe and the choices we make.

The good news is that doctors are human. The bad news is that many women (unconsciously) still place too much responsibility on the doctor. Yes, second opinions are more popular, but not enough questions are being asked.

It is time for women to shed this old belief and to value their doctor as their *partner* in health and well-being. You are being called to *know your body better than your doctor*. The feminine spirit within you knows, and will guide you to knowing what's normal for you and what's not. All you need to do is listen to your inner voice and become aware. It is simply a matter of paying attention and talking with other women. This helps you strengthen your inner power, so that in the event you need to consult a doctor, you are building on your own knowledge. No one can sway you from your own truth. Know your body and trust your instincts.

Recently, I had the opportunity to sit with several women, two of whom wished to have a baby and were having trouble conceiving. In the midst of this intimate conversation about conception, I asked one of them, "Do you know when you are ovulating?" She responded by telling me what her doctor told her about her cycle. I posed the question again. At first she looked at me as if I had three heads. Then I briefly explained that the vaginal fluids distinctively change when a woman ovulates. She was astonished!

The woman next to me dove right into the conversation and described the distinctions beautifully. It was really special watching her just beam with inner love as she explained her truth. You could feel her strength in the knowledge of her own body.

In my space with women, I enjoy creating conversations that enlighten them with a deeper sense of self. I find it *so* exciting and refreshing to see women step out of the so-called "horror stories" and to watch transformation occur before my very eyes. Nothing confirms the presence and the power of the feminine spirit more than witnessing its aliveness in the hearts of women.

I know that the feminine spirit is extremely

powerful, because I personally knew I was pregnant within twenty-four hours of each conception—long before my doctor knew. I didn't believe I needed a doctor to tell me what I already knew. I would simply receive my confirmation about four weeks later from a blood test and start my monthly exams thereafter. There are many, many women who have experienced the same inner knowing. You need not be a genius to know your body. Just be present with it, and you will discover incredible knowledge.

At times, we inherit beliefs based on what our mothers experienced in their own lives. For example, a woman's mother died of heart disease at forty-two years of age. The daughter unconsciously believed that she would also die of the same disease at age forty-two. Interestingly enough, she began to show signs that she was heading down the same path. One day, she expressed her concerns and fears to a relative, only to learn that her grandmother had always feared heart disease, though she had lived until the ripe old age of ninety-five. Although the grandmother did not die of heart disease, as a child she had witnessed the death of someone who did. The relative further explained that the woman's mother had been the first in the family to die of heart disease.

This knowledge was a breakthrough for the woman, who was approaching her fortieth birthday. She realized that the belief and fear she was carrying were not hers. She recalled conversations she'd had with her grandmother about her mother's childhood, of how her mother was not allowed to run very much, for fear she would have a heart attack. As the woman still mourned the death of her mother, she began to release her old beliefs and fears about heart disease. She realized that she had been holding herself back from being active, and not really living. She began to do all the things she longed to do, and all of her symptoms simply vanished. In time, she was able to forgive her grandmother for unintentionally passing on her fear to her daughter. After all, her grandmother had been just a child—and how traumatic it must have been to witness someone's death!

A powerful exercise for evaluating your beliefs is to begin to listen to your self-talk. Listen to what your mind is telling you over and over again. Chances are that much of what you hear does not apply to who you really are or your truest self. Take a week or two and pay close attention to what you hear.

Personally, I was amazed not only at the messages I was hearing, but at the staggering repetition that was enough to drive someone crazy! Writing these messages down allowed me to place them where they belonged: on paper, instead of in my mind! Simply by writing these down, I consciously acknowledged them. The need to hear such cruel words as "you're wasting time" silently faded away.

I wish I could say I've eliminated all of my negative mind chatter, but it is an ongoing process. However, I have managed to get rid of some of the most annoying chatter. The most challenging and perhaps the most necessary time for evaluating my beliefs is when things aren't flowing the way I'd like them to. It takes a conscious effort to constantly pay attention and focus on thought patterns that serve me.

I believe that keeping a journal is essential for personal growth, as it can expedite the process by facilitating clarity. If you have never kept a journal, this would be a perfect time to start one and record your findings. You will be amazed at what you find. It can be an exciting way of discovering any blocks you may have in your life as a result of beliefs that no longer serve you.

There is a wonderful computer journal that I use called "Seize the Day." This was given to me as a gift from a very special woman. I love this journal because it offers an active picture that changes every month. In addition, if I am in the month of May, for example, I can time-travel to the September seascape, where it might be raining! It is an absolutely beautiful and easy way to set the tone for self-expression. (Several family members can use this program, since it allows each person to choose his or her own password.) You can purchase the program through MAXCOM Inc., 4625 First Street, Suite 270, Pleasanton, CA 94566, 1-800-882-5658. When you call to order your program, please mention *In Honor of Women*, and $3.00 will be donated to WIN Against Breast Cancer.

As you record your thoughts, self-talk, and beliefs, see if you can think back to where or when they originated. Be sure to record this as well. Allow yourself to feel whatever emotion that comes forth. Know that this is a wonderful way to cleanse your heart of any criticism or negative belief that may have been passed on to you. Remember, you have the choice and the ability to change what you don't want. So when an unpleasant thought comes into your mind, you can choose to thank it for being there and then replace it with a positive thought. For example, you can change the thought, "I am so fat today," to "I love my body." Be creative with your positive affirmations. You will find that the more you do this, the happier you will be. Remember that you create what you believe. So if there is something that keeps reoccurring in your life, it is all the more reason to take a look at your beliefs that may be related to it. You can stop the pattern and be blessed with enlightenment. In addition, you may prevent the pattern from filtering down to future generations.

Allow yourself the opportunity to forgive the person who may have planted the idea of any negative belief pattern in you. Surround yourself with love and the white light of the divine feminine spirit. Imagine what it would feel like to feel only love for this person. After all, love is truly the only thing that anyone and everyone wants in life.

Once you have acknowledged and released any beliefs that no longer serve you, you can begin to create what you believe by focusing on a new belief. For example, one of my old beliefs was about not being good enough (which, by the way, is a belief that is usually passed on through several generations). I placed myself in the space of being good enough. "I am good enough. In fact, I am powerful and I make a difference in people's lives." This is what I use as a simple affirmation to keep me focused. Stepping into this space is much like putting on a new suit. It allows me to feel valuable and confident. I now know that the idea that I am good enough is no longer just a new belief, but it is truly a reality!

Creating what we believe is not difficult once we become clear about what we choose as new core beliefs. These new beliefs must serve to empower us as we invite truth into our lives. Since it is our beliefs that shape our reality, it is well worth the time to re-shape our outdated beliefs while creating the reality of our deepest desires.

Doing this inner work will transform you into being the you that you have always wanted to be! The gifts are within you.

Chapter 8

101 Ways to Honor Yourself as a Woman

The following poem is one of two beautiful contributions to this book written by Leslie Goldman. I personally was very excited to find such beautiful words written by a man. I encourage every woman to have a laminated copy posted on her refrigerator. You can purchase one by contacting Leslie at (619) 582-9669, c/o Enchanted Garden—USA, 6008 Arosa Street, San Diego, CA 92115.

BECAUSE SHE IS A WOMAN

In the infinite wonder of the life of every woman
is the moment to be celebrated
that she takes space,
that she learns to relax into taking space.

Space to be alone. Space to absolve.
Space to feel nothing but the ancient memory
that comes when she bathes alone,

hears the wispy sound of warm water moving
as she feels comfort she has made for herself,
as she does the things
that make her feel pretty in her own eyes.

This is space taken without guilt.
This is time taken she owes no one.
This is uncompromised, exquisitely selfish space
    that she takes
    because she is a woman.

A man is a gentle man when he knows
    what it means for a woman to take space.
A man has become a man when he feels honored
    when the woman he loves takes space.
He is honored when she says,
    "I'm taking space now."
A woman has become a woman
    when she takes space.

—LESLIE GOLDMAN
© 1987

It is so enjoyable to look at the possibilities and ways to honor yourself as a woman. The sky is the limit! I have created these ways as a starting point for you. I personally use this list as a reminder for myself, and I share it with you as ideas for creating your own list. I encourage you to read through the entire list and *highlight what stands out for you.* Then, choose one or more activity to do every week. Write them in your calendar a month or two in advance. Believe me, you will be continuously inspired to be consistent. I also encourage you to record your experiences. Feel free to use the pages in the back of this book specified for personal observations. Share this with your friends and encourage them to do the same. I celebrate with you, for I know you will find great happiness in honoring yourself!

1. Meditate fifteen to twenty minutes a day.
2. Surround yourself with your favorite music.
3. Take yourself to a movie.
4. Go to a park or the countryside and be one with nature.
5. Surround yourself with laughter and people who love you.
6. Visit a pet store filled with animals you can play with.
7. Buy yourself some fresh-cut flowers and place them in your environment.
8. Start a garden and witness what you can grow.
9. Visit with children and listen to what they have to teach you.

10. Acknowledge those around you who are angels, and the fact that you have brought them to you.
11. Purchase a beautiful piece of artwork for yourself.
12. Have your nails done.
13. Adorn yourself with your favorite perfume.
14. Take an aromatherapy bath.
15. Have a professional masseuse come to your home and give you a massage once a month.
16. Find a great book to read.
17. Keep a journal of your personal thoughts and feelings.
18. Find a form of exercise that is fun, and therefore effortless.
19. Take a class or a course that will add joy to your life.
20. Write down your inner dreams and desires. This affirms the possibility of making them happen.
21. Make an appointment with someone you have been longing to see.
22. Keep a log of all the small miracles that are taking place in your life.
23. Open your heart to your inner self and say "no" when you want to free yourself from any so-called "should."

24. Do a breast self-examination once a month.
25. Have your hair cut and styled.
26. Have a facial once a month.
27. Take time to pray and feel spiritually whole.
28. Thank yourself for the good that you do in the world.
29. Nourish yourself with what you consider to be quality foods.
30. Meet with a small group of women on a monthly basis and focus on the divine feminine spirit that mirrors each of them. Focus on the inner beauty of each individual.
31. Balance any complaint you may have in your life about yourself with a gift that you have to offer.
32. Make a list of the gifts you have to offer.
33. Make a list of what you want to receive in your life—emotionally, financially, physically, and spiritually.
34. Make a list of all your strengths and keep it in a place where you spend a lot of time.
35. Ask people who know you to share with you what they feel is special and beautiful about you. *(Children are great for this one!)*
36. Buy yourself fragranced candles and

enjoy the softness of the light they provide.

37. Adorn yourself only with clothes that make you feel like a million bucks!

38. Be spontaneous and do something you have always wanted to do but never made time for!

39. Take space proudly and without guilt!

40. Identify your purpose in life and the deep passion and love you hold within it.

41. Create a job for yourself that allows you to express your passion and your purpose. Watch yourself make a difference in the world.

42. Buy yourself something that you have always wanted.

43. Tell yourself that you are safe and no one can harm you.

44. Share your purpose and the excitement of it with others; they will in turn feel a stirring within and bring theirs forth as well.

45. Make a list of things that distinguish you as someone who makes a difference.

46. See yourself as powerful!

47. Be true to yourself and fill yourself with integrity.

48. Be proud of who you are and what you stand for!
49. Take note of this very moment and feel with all your senses. It is great to be alive!
50. Get rid of the "should" in your life by allowing yourself to say, "I surrender into the flow of life."
51. Hug the people you love.
52. Express what you feel.
53. Make a list of the most incredible things you have done in your life.
54. Make a list of the things you are grateful for.
55. Find a quiet and special place outside of your home where you can indulge and be one with yourself.
56. View your birthday as a celebration of wisdom.
57. Look into the possibilities of what you wish to create in your life, and then create!
58. Sing and dance as often as possible!
59. Become one with your sense of knowing; trust yourself.
60. Move forward into self-talk that empowers you.
61. Free yourself from any "guilts" by acknowledging that everything in life happens exactly as it is meant to.
62. Challenge yourself to find the gift in

what you consider to be a difficult situation.

63. Create a vision of your life that fulfills you.

64. Feel your vision with every cell of your body. Experience it fully.

65. At night, keep a pen and pad of paper next to your bed. If you are awakened with thoughts, write them down.

66. Be in tune with your spirit, mind, and body.

67. Whenever possible, sit with a full moon and allow your body to be permeated by the light. This is one of the most relaxing things to do. Find a quiet place to sit under a full moon, much like the way you would sit under the sun, and envision the light cascading into your body until you see your body as a beam of brilliant light. I personally have found this to be very grounding and soothing, particularly during premenstrual days.

68. Allow a beloved to love you and give to you.

69. Fill your house with colors you love!

70. Call a high school friend and reminisce about good times from the past.

71. Wear only colors that you love!

72. Throw away (or give away) the clothes you have in sizes that haunt you, and free yourself from the "what-if's"!

73. Dress for yourself as an expression of who you are, and feel your own empowerment.

74. Share wonderful stories about your life with others so they, too, can find value within themselves.

75. Buy a camera and take pictures of special moments and things that you love: people, animals, etc.

76. Buy yourself new makeup and throw out the old!

77. Take a special trip and discover a new place, and perhaps a new culture.

78. Study people, especially women, and see how they mirror you and your gifts.

79. Find an old tree and sit under it. Admire its beauty and imagine what it would say to you if it could only speak of times long gone.

80. Read one of your favorite books to a child.

81. Surround yourself with individuals older than yourself and listen to some of the gifts they have to offer in the realm of wisdom and experience. See it as a privilege to be in their presence.

82. Take a stand and express what you believe in.

83. Whenever possible, take a nap and allow your body and mind to rest because you deserve it.

84. Send your mother flowers on *your* birthday as a special acknowledgment for having had you, because without her, you wouldn't be here!

85. Treat yourself to a pedicure once a month.

86. Add almond or coconut oil to your hair and leave it in overnight. After shampooing, you will love the softness of your hair.

87. Witness and experience the happiness and beauty of new lives by visiting a hospital nursery, affirming that beautiful babies are born every day.

88. Create a special project with other women.

89. Treat yourself to a women's retreat at least once a year.

90. Purchase a special piece of jewelry for yourself.

91. Take yourself and someone you love on a picnic.

92. Go to an opera and experience the depth of music. Allow yourself to be moved by greatness!

93 Believe that your body is beautiful exactly as it is in its present state.

94. Know your body sexually, for no one will know it better! Be proud to be a woman.

95. Take your vitamins daily!

96. Develop friendships with men who truly have your best interest in mind.

97. Take an old piece of jewelry and ask your jeweler to help you design something new.

98. Buy new clothes for lounging that are soft and comfortable.

99. Develop hobbies that are truly enjoyable and playful.

100. Plant a rose garden and take a few minutes every day to take in its beauty.

101. Celebrate your life with laughter and love, and share it with all who cross your path. Know that everyone who crosses your path has a gift, a message just for you to receive!

I have personally experienced many of these and have found a great deal of joy with every one. Life is fuller as I have learned to open my heart to receiving.

Chapter 9   Defining Your Purpose and Living It

Like many children of God, I'd always had a sense of knowing that I was meant for greatness. But it wasn't until I was healing from breast cancer that I began to clearly define my life purpose. Had it not been for this life-threatening disease, I would still be searching for a way to make a difference in this world, which had always been my intention. As a result of this disease, I was able to ultimately express my love for people by creating this book and sharing much of what I have learned.

Prior to this turning point in my life, I had committed myself to writing a book for women about their self-image in regard to fashion, with Marie Taylor, a ghostwriter. Little did I know that this was to be my training ground for writing.

Breast cancer soon became my real teacher, which brought out my inner confidence in not only my writing, but also in being far more self-expressive with my purpose. The healing that has evolved with this experience continues to give me great joy, and it feeds my soul. Clearly my purpose is to reach millions of women all over the world and offer my message as a gift, before illness ever emerges as their teacher.

I believe that everyone on this planet has a purpose in life that is unique and distinctive. Each of us is blessed with special talents and attributes. Focusing on your purpose gives you the opportunity to live through your heart and to contribute your gifts to the universe.

You need not face your own mortality in order to define what your purpose in life is. I believe that if each of us allowed ourselves the opportunity to look at our gifts and to live our dreams, there would be fewer people getting sick.

Look into your heart and see what your dream is about. A dream is a powerful vision. No dream is too small. Be willing to explore the world of possibilities that surround your dream. What do you envision yourself doing? Where do you see yourself living? How do you see yourself being? Whom do you wish to experience this with? Once you have fulfilled your dream, how will it help you make a difference in the world? Let your mind's eye see every little detail. Now take your journal and write out everything about your dream. Be as specific as possible. In time, you may find yourself adding more details as you allow your creativity to flow.

A dear friend of mine, Lenda Travis Heinaman, once said that God would not give us dreams if they weren't possible. How right she was, for today she is the proud mother of a beautiful baby boy. After years of wanting a child, Lenda and her husband were able to adopt this very special little being. Dreams, without a doubt, do come true.

Sometimes a dream can remain trapped within the mind because there's attachment to the belief that it is only a dream. So, one can have a dream, yet unconsciously create blocks to it, or reasons for not manifesting it into reality. For example, a woman was once asked about her dream. Her face lit up like a child in a candy store. She took a breath and smiled as she shifted into relief. This woman had been ill with various ailments for quite some time. Taking the opportunity to discuss her dream allowed her to momentarily step out of her physical pain. She said that her dream in life was to travel to different parts of the world and experience the people and their various cultures. When asked if and where she had traveled in the past, she sadly stated that she had never left the state in which she had been born. She explained that her health issues were the reason she didn't travel.

It was clear that her dream was magnificent to her, yet her focus had always been on how sick she was. When asked if she was willing to look at the possibilities of fulfilling her dream, she answered "yes." In her voice, there was a sense of both excitement and fear (which, by the way, come from the same place). Her therapist suggested that the excitement of planning a little trip might help her step into what she really desired and help her feel better. Then her therapist brought a calendar to her and asked her about the possibility of arranging her first trip. She was simply overwhelmed with joy and agreed to take this step.

Today she is quite a traveler, and sends her friends postcards from all over the world. It was her willingness to explore that moved her out of old patterns and into creating a whole new life for herself. As a result, living her dream became much bigger than her fear and health issues.

When we place a lot of importance or attention on what we don't want, we allow it to become bigger than what we do want. This creates a pattern of events that keeps us stuck. Energy flows where attention goes. It is important that your energy flows toward what you do want rather than what you don't want.

Stepping into the world of vast possibilities may seem frightening at first because there is a natural desire to stay with what is familiar and known. Yet, we know in our heart of hearts that we are truly limiting ourselves. Acknowledging our fears allows us to own them and embrace them as being OK!

The truth is that *surrendering into the unknown* is a great way to release that which is in your way. Quite simply, we often base our trust on what we know, and this is our greatest limitation! This is what causes us unconsciously to re-create the same issues or patterns in our lives. This is what causes us to feel stuck, and we suffer a great deal as a result.

The moment I personally surrendered into the unknown, I released *my way* of doing things, along with my control. I realized it was far more exciting to let go of what I knew and embrace a much larger plan. I got out of my own way! The key for me is staying within my own joy by honoring my desires and wishes, as well as staying open to the possibilities that surround me. I also believe that everyone who crosses my path has a gift and a powerful message for me to receive, and I have one to give them. We are here to serve one another. For me, every encounter is a blessed encounter.

Releasing my control was—and at times still is—very challenging. Yet, this conscious exercise is what allows me to live my purpose, and realize that my purpose is bigger than any fear or concern I may have had in the past. I have also released whatever was blocking me by placing all of my energy on bringing forth my message. So, during the five years of personal study, research, and lots of inner work, all for the sake of my growth and this book, I experienced movement. It felt like the whole world shifted when, in fact, it was I who shifted where I was placing my energy and began to trust. Suddenly, I began to receive calls from people who wanted to hear me speak, and who supported this book as if it were their own project.

I feel so blessed. The universe supports me in unexpected ways, allowing me the opportunity to speak on many subjects which I am so passionate about. So, I am excited to say that I truly don't know what the next moment or the next day will bring.

When I find myself determined to do things *my way*, I find myself miserable and stressing out. This is my cue to stop and release, and get back into the flow of life. Who wants to fight to make things happen when they can happen effortlessly?

Trusting in the flow of life is reflective of the divine feminine spirit and serves us abundantly in living our purpose. This trust comes from self-love. Whatever holds us back from living within our heart's desire does not come from love. For example, feelings of guilt, self-criticism, self-denial, and self-deprivation do not come from love. They are ego-based. The ego is far more interested in looking good than being true to the self. As you surrender, you are opening the door that has always been there for you and transformation occurs immediately.

Just for a moment, picture God giving you a gift. (Please use whatever term you prefer if God is not appropriate for you. It may be Buddha, the Infinite Creator, your higher power, or something else.) It is a gift you cannot see with your eyes, but you are deeply moved by its presence. Coming from God, you know that it is pure and sacred. It is the gift of self. *Every time you diminish yourself and your truth, you begin to tear it down, therefore shattering a piece of God himself.*

Surrendering allows us to trust that we are being guided every moment of our lives. It is a most natural process to live our purpose. *You know you are living your purpose when you begin to receive all that you need for your process.* Things seem to just flow with ease and fall right at your feet. It is a journey filled with passion and, most of all, love. If you are not in love with what you are doing, you are not living your purpose. Remember, there is no right or wrong. It is simply a matter of choice and what you want in life.

In addition to defining your purpose, make a list of 101 things that you desire to receive to help you fulfill your purpose in life. You will be amazed at how this list will initiate movement. It is a wonderful exercise, as it brings forth imagination and excitement. *Make a commitment to yourself and grant that your wishes come true!* Being aware of what you are receiving will serve as a significant reminder that you are on your path and that you are living your purpose!

There is no greater joy than that of living your purpose. It simply does not serve you or the universe to hold yourself back. The more you focus on your intention, the more opportunities will present themselves to you. You will receive confirmation by experiencing so-called "coincidences." I don't believe in mere coincidence. I do believe that what we view as coincidence is pure confirmation or support given to us that we may effortlessly fulfill our life's plan, or what we are here on earth to do. We, as human beings, are far more powerful than we give ourselves credit for. Awakening to who we are propels us with great speed through our fears, so that we can better understand our magnificence and shine our light brilliantly.

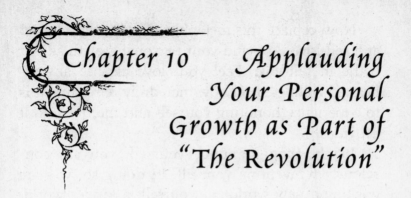

Chapter 10   *Applauding Your Personal Growth as Part of "The Revolution"*

There is no doubt in my mind that a powerful yet gentle movement is occurring at this moment. Unlike other movements in the past, this one is not about fighting. In fact, it is about moving in a direction that brings forth life and a quality of life. It is about saving the lives of women today. It is about change occurring for the sake of our future generations. And it is about acknowledging who we are as women, and honoring our personal growth. How wonderful it is to participate in such a movement!

It's as if we have been thirsty for so long that we've forgotten what water tastes like. In fact, we have fought for water for so long that many of us have died from the lack of it. Now, we suddenly remember how refreshing it is to drink, and how wonderful it is to be cleansed by it. We are awakening to all of our memories. Now we realize that we will thirst no more. All the water we ever wanted and needed was here all along.

Now, replace this metaphor of water with honor and self-love. Applaud your personal growth as you bathe in self-love. Feel your love cleanse any ill-hearted feelings. Feel how incredibly refreshing it is to experience honoring yourself and the freedom it provides.

In choosing to honor yourself, you are consciously reinventing yourself. In doing so, you are creating a new world for yourself: a kinder world, one that respects you and holds you dear.

I will be the first to say that this conscious change does not occur without growing pains. When I first got in touch with the possibility of honoring myself, I was concerned about losing some of my friends. I was worried that the people in my life would see me as selfish or self-centered. Honoring myself would mean that I'd need to say "no" more often and not commit myself to *so* much. I wondered what people would think of me. Truly, my biggest concern was about disappointing others and how this would affect my life.

I found it paramount to ask myself: Who am I really committed to? Am I committed to my ego and looking good through all of my so-called "obligations"? Or am I committed to my own truth? Frankly, I grew tired of trying to please everyone. I made the commitment to trust my heart even when it was the most difficult thing to do. I realized that my life depended on making this change. And I believed in my heart that true friends would remain and the quality of my life would improve a thousandfold.

Because of the happiness I've experienced through honoring myself, my life today is far richer and more fulfilling. True friends have remained friends, while some casual acquaintances have fallen away. I believe it is important, however, to give people the space and time they need to adjust to the "new you." This means being OK with people who don't understand what you're up to. It means releasing any judgments you may have of them, as well as those you *think* they have of you!

Every time you consciously say "yes" to your heart instead of your ego, you are breaking through and reinventing yourself. Every time you let go of an overwhelming sense of guilt for taking care of your needs, you are also breaking through and reinventing yourself. So the guilt diminishes and then disappears. This process takes conscious effort, and it is not always comfortable. However, the rewards usually outweigh the temporary discomfort. It's like learning to walk again. Those first steps are the most challenging!

In your journal, write about some of these first baby steps. Track what feels monumental and almost impossible to do. Write down how you honor yourself each day. For example, today I honored myself by simply creating a list of ways I will please myself. This is a great vehicle that can be used as a reminder on days that appear to be less than perfect! So, if you're having a bad day, it will serve you to review lists from the past. It will surely put a smile on your face to look at what has pleased you in the past, and give you a warm feeling that radiates self-love. Taking just a moment to reflect on something you wrote about in your journal is honoring yourself.

One of the most monumental issues for me was to allow myself to continue to work on this project since it is my passion, and to let go of guilt in regard to my family. Any working woman is well aware that it feels like quite a juggling act to meet the demands of a job while raising children and keeping a household organized and running smoothly. It would defeat my purpose to make myself wrong while working on such a project! Eliminating guilt allowed me the freedom to work happily from the heart. I found it most helpful to get clear about my needs first in my journal, and then communicate them to John, as part of honoring myself. "Journaling" allowed me to see clearly that balance could be achieved if I viewed taking care of my family's needs as a way to stay grounded.

This perspective allowed me to be completely present at times when I was needed, without feeling as if I were being interrupted from my work. And my feeling of being grounded was a form of honoring myself. Without it, I felt I might lose sight of the things that are important in my life. My work might become all that I would have, and by itself would not be totally fulfilling.

Applaud your personal growth by keeping a running dialogue of the ways you call forth your self-love. This will help you stay focused and remind you of what truly makes you happy.

PART TWO

WOMEN ARE BIGGER THAN BREAST CANCER!

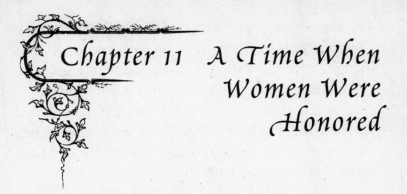

Chapter 11 A Time When Women Were Honored

Although there are other time periods and cultures in our history of civilization when women were honored, I wish to acknowledge the Cherokee, an American Indian tribe, for their reverence toward women.

Interestingly, Cherokee women had more rights and power during the seventeenth and eighteenth centuries than did European women. A Cherokee woman could marry whomever she chose. This man would build her a house, and the house was considered her personal property. It was also understood that the children were hers. Her brothers would help her rear the children. To obtain a divorce, all she had to do was pack her husband's clothes in a bag and set it outside the door. She was then free to marry again, even someone outside her tribe. For example, she could marry a white man if she desired. The Cherokee woman was treated as a valued partner.

It was through the Cherokee mother that children gained clan identity, which afforded them citizenship.

The mother was the center of the children's world. Children were considered to be very special. It was thought to be demeaning to show a lack of respect for a child's dignity, and hitting them was not allowed.

Specific areas were set aside for each woman and her daughters to grow vegetables. As farmers, they were one with the earth and her sacredness. Meals were cooked by the women.

During my research, I had the privilege of meeting Maye Myatt, a lovely woman whose ancestors were Cherokee. It was fascinating to recapture some of her fondest childhood memories with her. Listening to her recount stories about her paternal grandmother, I could sense the joy she must have experienced as a child.

Maye recalled, "The Cherokee people were a very peaceful and family-oriented people. The women would band together with all their children and tell wonderful stories. If one woman had a skill, she would teach it to all the children. The women believed in working hard and teaching the children everything they knew. There was a wonderful sense of love and respect for all the women and children. The men were very proud. I remember my father telling me, 'Because you are an Indian, you are expected to excel. You have to be better than most and be proud to be an Indian.'"

It is interesting and exciting to me that the native women viewed their bleeding time as most sacred. In her book, *Sister Moon Lodge,* Kisma Stepanich clearly describes the depth of this sacredness, and the power and mystery of menstruation. She explains that the native women had small huts away from the main section of the village. They would gather to share their experience and to share the pain of menstrual cramps. Within these huts, better known as Moon Lodges, they would sing and prepare soothing herbal teas to help each other with the pain. I find it fascinating that the women would stay in these lodges for several days until their bleeding had stopped. During this time the children were taken care of by their uncles and sometimes the wise crones.

The wise crones had their own lodges where they shared stories and brought forth great wisdom, which allowed them to guide their tribes. These women were highly respected not only for their wisdom, but also for their gifts of spiritualism, nurturing, and love. Their wisdom blessed the tribe with great abundance, and they were truly honored. The wise crones or grandmothers were always welcome to join the other women at the Moon Lodges.

These Native American women believed in the sacred connection between women, earth, and moon. They believed that the phases of the moon were directly reflective of the phases or cycles of a woman. All of the women in the tribe bled together around the same time.

Let me explain further. The lunar cycle consists of twenty-eight days, beginning with:

1. The new or crescent moon; then
2. The waxing moon;
3. The full moon;
4. The waning phase; and
5. The dark moon, when the moon is not visible at all.

With the new moon, a woman's body feels lighter since water retention is very little and the womb is no longer carrying the blood. As women, we also feel lighter emotionally, eager to love, play, and enjoy life. We feel a wonderful sense of energy.

As the moon begins to wax or increase in size, our bodies reflect this change. Once the moon reaches fullness, we feel full and swollen also.

Having made this connection has led me to celebrate my cycle and view it with fresh eyes. This new understanding has diminished many of my physical complaints in regard to bloating and cramping. I now look at the full moon with gratitude and smile, knowing of a deeper connection within.

Entering the dark moon phase, we begin to feel darkness within ourselves. If we don't receive conception from life's seed, our wombs begin to bleed. Our wombs weep as our hearts do. This is why we feel depressed when we bleed. It's because we bleed for life, and when life is not present, we are sad. We feel extremely sensitive at this time since our hormones are changing. It is our sacred time to stop and to realize our own power—the power that we were born with. During this time our sense of knowing or intuition is truly heightened.

It is specifically at this point that we must take time to pamper ourselves. By doing so, we are telling the world that we see ourselves as most important, before taking care of anyone or anything else. We are reclaiming our divinity.

We have much to learn from the ancient native women. Our bleeding is not a curse. It is a time to honor our bodies. We cannot expect men to understand or honor us if we don't understand and honor this very precious gift. When men bleed, it's usually because they are hurt, and they can possibly die from the loss of blood. Yet, as women, we bleed month after month for several days at a time, and we do not die. *We bleed for life! We represent life and we give life.*

Another beautiful book that reminds us of the ways of our ancient native sisters is *Daughters of Copper Women* by Anne Cameron. I wept like a child during certain parts of this book, feeling my connection with the ancient woman and her evolution. I felt a strong connection with the divine feminine spirit deep within my heart.

The experience of writing this book has led me

to understand more fully my power as a woman. The ways of the ancient woman live within me and cannot be forgotten. I cherish my bleeding time and its sacredness. I take time for aromatherapy baths and to acknowledge the vital importance of honoring myself. My own cycle reflects itself as a mirror of the cycles or phases of the moon.

Can you imagine taking several days each month to be with other women in honor of our sacred bleeding? Just for a moment, think of how incredibly refreshing it would be to leave everything behind and allow our bodies to rest during this sensitive time! In today's world, this would seem like a mini vacation. I know I would certainly come back renewed, refreshed, and ready to take on the world!

In reality, many of us may not be able to completely remove ourselves for days at a time. However, simply having an awareness of our needs during this time can help us change the way we treat ourselves on these days. For example, I have shared this information with my husband, and now he understands my need for quiet time. He may choose to take the children to a movie while I curl up with a book or get a massage.

For women who no longer bleed, I encourage you to take time to celebrate your wisdom by sharing it with younger women. It is so welcomed! Share your stories with us so we can learn from you. You have *so* much to offer us! You have laid the foundation for those of us who follow. Celebrate your wisdom, your love, and your passions!

Looking at times when women were honored brings us closer to feeling what it is to be honored in today's world. In *Sister Moon Lodge*, Kisma writes a beautiful chapter in honor of our ancient grandmothers called "The Voice of the Grandmothers." I share with you a very powerful section of it, which moves me every time I read it.

"There was a time," [the grandmother] begins, "when women were honored. We kept the peace. We kept the unity of the village together. There was a time when we gathered together and allowed our musings to be heard and discussed. There was a time when our voices were sought. Our words guided the welfare of the people. We lived in the women's ways of power and nurturance.

"But in the past men grew jealous of this natural gift of power that we held. They joined together seeking to overpower it. They had a long fight on their hands!"

The crowd cheered. The old woman continued. "Yes, they had a long fight on their hands. In fact, in order for them to be victorious they had to murder us!" Silence. Eyes closed. Tears flowed. Moans of sorrow.

"Why?" the old woman beseeched the sky. "Why would a mighty God allow his people to be so brutal? What would they gain by throwing the partnership off balance?

"These men, these tribes, did not stop and ask themselves these questions. But the grandmothers were given the answers, and as we came forward to give warning of such actions, our voices were silenced. Now we have become weak, separated, ignorant.

"Well, I will not remain weak any longer. I will not stand alone. I am not ignorant. I call to my sisters. I call to the virgins, the mothers, the grandmothers, the crones, all women of every age, wake up. Wake up and stand strong and firm in your power. Our voice is needed. Our experience and understanding of relationships and the partnership of life, the balance of the two primal energies of life—female and male—are gravely needed.

"We must stand up and shout at the top of our lungs: We will not have things killed. We will not have the forests cut down. We will not have our waters polluted. We will not let our people go homeless, [or let] our children starve. We will not stand for war. These are unacceptable now! Let us change the world. Let us enact the world vision of peace and unity and balance and healing. Let us begin now."

Chapter 12   Our Sacred Sisterhood

When I think of our sisterhood I envision women of all ages, from all walks of life, standing, receiving one another as part of each other. I see women of every race and every nation standing tall, proud to be women. I see our hearts all linked together as one, forming infinite circles. The first circle wraps around the earth herself. The second circle wraps around just inside the border of the earth. Each circle gets slightly smaller until the circles reach the center of our Mother Earth. The center of Mother Earth is her heart, which is the heart of every woman. Our sacred sisterhood is the heart of life. This is where it all begins.

There is no greater power than that of women who come together to honor each other. During our time together, we share compassion, understanding, nurturing, laughter, creativity, excitement, and most of all love. We have the ability to experience all of this and more over just a cup of tea! The gifts we bring to one another are incredibly magnificent. We have so much to learn from each other! Sharing our stories gives us the opportunity to share our wisdom.

I marvel at the stories I hear from older women. I was recently privileged to hear the powerful words of Miep Gies, a phenomenal woman who hid Anne Frank and her family and friends in an attic for more than two years. I was taken by her presence long before I heard her speak. She told us, "You must act if injustice happens. We should not wait for leaders to make the world a better place. We should make this change now in our homes and in our schools." I can still hear her deep voice and the incredible strength it carries. My eyes filled with tears as I listened to her tell of her love for the Franks and all of humanity.

There's so much to learn from our wise elders. There's something magical about grandmothers and their stories. I love to phone my grandmother, who is ninety-four. She lives in Italy, so she keeps her stories short, but it's wonderful to hear her chuckle about our times together. I often imagine what it must be like for her to be the last survivor of a family of fifteen children. I admire and honor her for her faith, strength, and wisdom.

As you share your stories with women of all ages, focus on the discoveries you made along the way. Remember the strength you received in moments of darkness and inspire your sister to remem-

ber hers. This is what brings forth self-love in others. Choose to raise the consciousness of the divine
feminine spirit by just *being* with someone who is
experiencing a difficult time. Listen to her and learn
from her experience. This comforts her in a way she
least expects. Acknowledge what she teaches you.

Photo by Debra Martin

Four generations:
Anna Campobasso Dicillo, my grandmother;
Grace Dicillo Togo, my mother;
Arianna Crawley, my daughter; and myself.

Recently, my friend Janna asked me something that I'm often asked: "What do you say to someone who tells you they are facing a life-threatening disease?" Janna told me she had received a call from a woman who had been diagnosed as having cancer. Janna had been surprised to hear from her, since it had been a while since they had talked. The news left her feeling uncertain about how she could help.

My response was, "What a privilege it is that she chose you as a friend to share this with. Know that she found comfort in just picking up the phone and reaching out to you. You were there, and there is no doubt that she is grateful for this. It is only human to wish for magical words at times like this. The best thing you can do is just *be* with her by calling her and letting her know you support her. Focus on who she is and not her illness. It will be a great break for her to reminisce about old times or to find laughter with you. This can help her see herself as being bigger than the disease."

I share this because I found it healthier to not involve some of my dearest friends in my healing. Although they meant well, they constantly placed their energy in wanting to know what the doctors said about the cancer, instead of supporting my healing plan. I did not want to place *any* energy into the disease. It was clear to me that in order to heal, I had to focus all of my energy on my healing, and step right into being well. Unfortunately, this is not easy to express, nor do I feel it is something that should be given any energy, *while* one is healing. So, it was OK for me to not involve some of my friends for the sake of saving my life. I know that my friends love me and wanted the same for me.

My family was extremely supportive of my healing plan. I gained tremendous strength from their allowing me to work my plan with very little questioning. Their trust in me gave me the strength and courage to do what I had to do. Several months after my healing process had come to a close both Mom and Papa shared with me that they in turn felt strengthened by watching me work my plan. They played an extremely important part in my healing by allowing me the space and time I needed, and helping out by watching my children and cooking meals. Their unconditional love empowered me to feel stronger and healthier than ever!

I believe that focusing on the healing rather than the illness can ultimately make or break someone's recovery process through unconscious influence. If we allow ourselves to be overcome by the ugliness and horror of a disease, and all the negative experiences that others may have had, we don't stand a chance of healing ourselves. Energy *must* be placed on healing the spirit and the mind; then hopefully the body will follow.

So, if you have a friend, sister, daughter, mother, grandmother, niece, or granddaughter with a health problem, placing your love and your energy in her spirit can only strengthen your bond. Your soul will be enriched by the experience. Don't let all of the other "stuff" get in the way of her spirit.

A very special friend of mind, Sister Joann Heinritz, asks a wonderful question: "How is your heart?" This is a perfect way to help those who are dealing with a health issue prioritize what truly matters. It is more soothing to ask this than to ask how they're feeling—particularly if you know they may not be feeling up to par.

I strongly encourage all women to take a look inside and see where you might feel a sense of separation from other women. If you do sense any, take note and ask—perhaps before meditation—what this is about. Listen for the answer. Regardless of how slight or how strong the feeling is, I believe it needs to be acknowledged so it can heal. A feeling of separation from other women is reflective of a separation within the self.

Stepping into the space of self-love allows us to forgive and release anything or anyone from emotional bondage. There simply is no place for judgment, fault, or guilt. These feelings create an energy that will reflect back to you in one manner or another. Envision this energy and transform it into white light. Contentment will revisit your life, and you will reconnect with the part of yourself that felt separated.

In reality, we are more alike than we are different. Yet it is also important to recognize that each of us is on our own path. Yes, there are different beliefs, different lifestyles, different voices, and so forth, but we all stem from the same sacred place: the heart.

Be true to your heart and know that you are a mirror to all the women of the world.

Chapter 13

A Gift to Yourself

One of the greatest gifts you can give yourself is to focus on your breast health by doing a breast self-examination each month. This book would not be complete without a simple guide to help you achieve this. I believe that this is at the heart of honoring ourselves as women.

When we take time to learn about our bodies, we can then identify a pattern of what is normal and what is not. This pattern of normalcy varies from woman to woman, since no two bodies are exactly alike. This is why it is important to establish your own normalcy baseline. For example, some women experience breast tenderness only prior to menstruating, while others experience tenderness before and during their menses. I know a woman who experiences tenderness as part of her daily life, and she is past her menopausal years.

By learning what is normal for you, you will create a sense of peacefulness. You will feel confident and self-assured. This is one of the many things we can do to help us feel in control in regard to our breast health. When we choose to take full responsibility for our breast health, we gently tell ourselves that we care and love ourselves. We place ourselves in a very clear and positive state of mind.

Many women don't realize that, although more women are being diagnosed with breast cancer, the percentage of survivors has also increased as a result of early detection. This is the key to surviving the disease. And this is why breast self-examination is *so* important.

Through the Breast Care Center, the Foundation for Advancement in Breast Care has developed a program called "Pearls of Wisdom," dedicated to encouraging and inspiring women to practice early detection of breast cancer. Its symbol is a ten-millimeter pearl on a pink ribbon, representing the size of a potentially curable breast cancer.

The program promotes the following three-step breast health plan:

+ Routine mammograms
+ Monthly breast self-exam
+ An annual clinical breast exam by a
  health professional who responds
  appropriately to symptoms.

Women who attend a Pearls of Wisdom presentation are encouraged to pledge themselves to this three-step health plan. Those who do receive their own pearl and ribbon.

I am honored to wear my ribbon and pearl because it gives men and women an opportunity to ask about its significance. Most people are aware of the different colored ribbons being worn today and what they stand for. However, the presence of a pearl is something they haven't seen, and it gives a tangible idea of the size of a potentially curable breast cancer. I think the pearl is a brilliant symbol, since it prompts immediate conversations and leads to increased awareness.

For more information about the Pearls of Wisdom program, contact the Breast Care Center at St. Joseph Medical Plaza, 505 S. Main Street, Suite 820, Orange, CA 92668; (714) 569-0318, x238; fax (714) 569-0215.

Many women have asked me, "What am I looking for while I am examining my breast? My breasts are very lumpy so it's difficult to tell what's normal and what is not. What does cancer feel like? Does it hurt?"

Many women perceive their breasts as being lumpy. When I talk about establishing a baseline of what is normal for you, I am talking about what you consider to be lumpy, for example. A regular monthly breast self-exam helps you distinguish what feels the same month after month, and any changes that might occur in size, texture, density, or appearance. The key is to identify any change and consult your physician.

In April 1996, Advanced Technology Laboratories (ATL) announced that the FDA had approved its premarket approval submission for ultrasound imaging of breast tumors. The newly approved breast ultrasound procedure, when used in conjunction with mammography and physical examination, will help physicians decide whether a biopsy is necessary for suspicious breast lesions. ATL's high-definition imaging (HDI) may reduce the number of biopsies performed by 40 percent or more. In a study of 700,000 women in the U.S., as many as 80 percent of the lumps found in women who underwent a breast biopsy were found to be benign. This new technology can help avoid biopsies and the anxiety women experience with a surgical procedure.

This is truly a great advancement, since it can eliminate the anxiety, pain, and expense of a biopsy. It can also eliminate unnecessary scarring and the emotional feelings that go along with it. The information may also assist in reducing the fear many women have of the "what-if's," and inspire them to follow the three-step breast health plan.

The American Cancer Society offers women the Special Touch Breast Health Program, one of many informative and successful programs. I was privileged to participate in this program, which taught me how to do a breast self-exam as well as how to teach it to others. To demonstrate what cancerous lumps feel like, the facilitators used silicone breast models with different substances carefully distributed in and around the bags of silicone gel. Each substance was a different size and texture. For example, there was one tiny, hard, beady substance. Another was a spongy substance with a hard center, which reminded me of the lump that had been present in my breast. To me, the center of my lump felt like a small pearl.

The purpose of using the models was to find the foreign substances with our fingerpads while practicing the techniques of a breast self-exam. The substances were not visible from the top of the breast model since the plastic coating was flesh-colored, but you could easily see them when you flipped the model upside down. These models are very helpful in teaching women what to feel for.

In cooperation with the American Cancer Society, I am proud to share with you on the following pages a simple, illustrated, step-by-step method called the "Seven P's," which will guide you in doing a breast self-exam.

Remember to set aside a day solely for the purpose of honoring yourself. For example, it might be a day that you get your hair or nails done. Make it a time for yourself, a time of relaxation and pampering. For women who are menstruating, it is recommended that you examine your breasts three to five days *after* your menses. For women who are menopausal or post-menopausal, it is recommended that you choose the same day of each month so it's easy to remember.

This is your gift to yourself. In time, it will seem no different than brushing your teeth! I hope you will teach this to your daughters and granddaughters. Give them a head start in breast health and the beauty of loving and knowing every part of their bodies.

THE "SEVEN P'S"

POSITIONS

Positions for Visual Inspection

The purpose of inspecting your breasts is to familiarize yourself with their general appearance so you will know what is normal for you and you can detect changes if they occur.

Always inspect your breasts in good lighting. Sometimes you may need to adjust the lighting to show subtle contour changes such as dimpling.

Visual inspection is performed in four positions standing or sitting in front of a mirror. In each position, look for changes in contour and shape of the breasts, color and texture of the skin and nipple. Also notice whether there is evidence of discharge from the nipples.

1. **Upright,** with arms relaxed at your sides (Fig. 1),

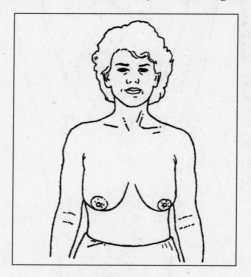

Figure 1

"The Seven P's BSE Guidelines" are reprinted from *Breast Self-Examination: A New Approach*, American Cancer Society, California Division, May 1992.

2. with **arms raised** above your head
   (Fig. 2),

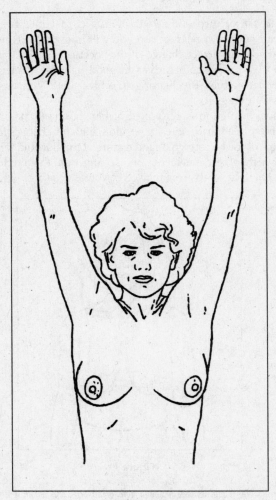

Figure 2

3. with **hands on your hips** pressing in while you
   contract your chest muscles (Fig. 3), and

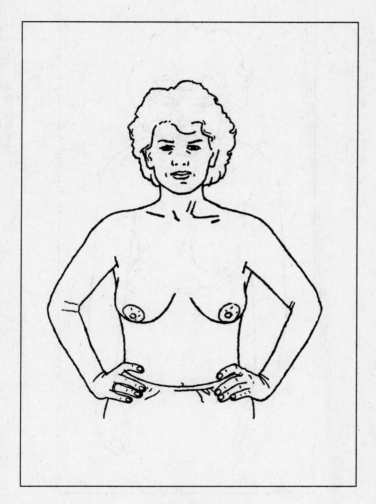

Figure 3

4. **bending forward** with arms relaxed at your sides (Fig. 4).

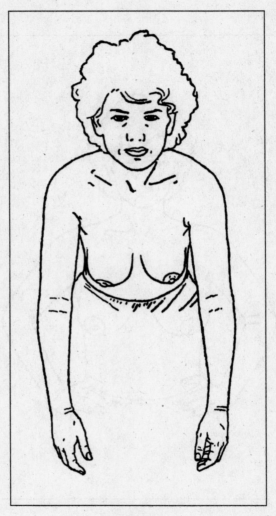

Figure 4

Positions for Palpation: Side-lying and Flat

By palpating your breasts, you can familiarize yourself with how they feel so you can detect a change if it occurs. The more familiar you become with your normal breast tissue, the more likely you will be to find the small, subtle—and more likely curable—abnormality. Most changes are benign.

Palpation is performed lying down. Use your left hand to palpate the right breast, while holding your right arm at a right angle to the rib cage, with the elbow bent. Repeat the procedure on the other side.

Women with small breasts ("A" cup or smaller) can examine their breasts while lying **flat** on their backs with a pillow or folded towel placed under the shoulder of the side with the breast to be examined (Fig. 5).

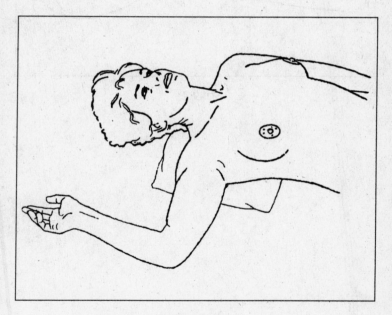

Figure 5

Women with large breasts ("B" cup or larger) may find the **side-lying** position especially helpful in exposing the upper outer quadrant of the breast. Lie on the side opposite the breast being examined. Your shoulder on the same side as the breast to be examined should rotate back to the flat surface (Fig. 6).

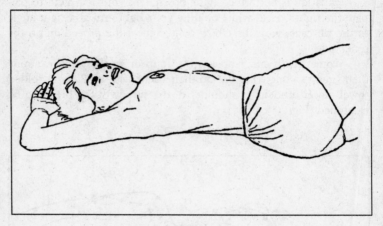

Figure 6

PERIMETER

The perimeter of the area to be examined should include all breast tissue. This area is bounded by a line that extends vertically from the middle of the axilla (armpit) to the rib just beneath the breast and continues horizontally along the underside of the breast to the mid sternum (middle of the breast bone). It continues up the mid sternum to the clavicle (collarbone), and along the lower border of the clavicle to the shoulder and back to the mid axilla (Fig 7).

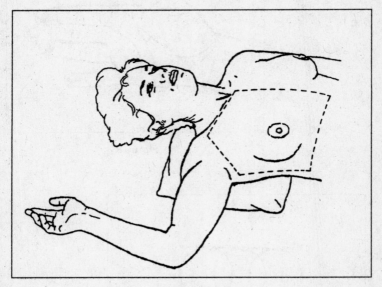

Figure 7

PALPATION TECHNIQUE WITH PADS

Palpation is performed with the **pads** of the fingers (Fig 8). Move your fingers (three or four) in small circles about the size of a dime (Fig. 8a).

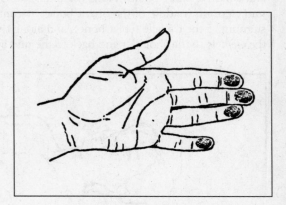

Figure 8

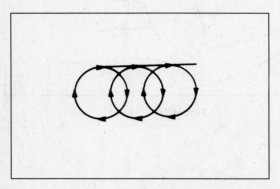

Figure 8a

PRESSURE

Since tumors are found at any level of the breast, you should examine the entire volume of breast tissue. Apply varying levels of pressure (light, medium and firm) to each spot palpated. Figure 9 illustrates a moderate amount of pressure. To apply firm pressure, compress the tissue until you can feel your ribs. The normal thickening of the inframammary ridge should not be mistaken for an abnormality.

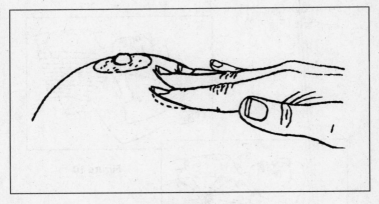

Figure 9

PATTERNS OF SEARCH

It is important that you palpate the breast in a systematic way and that you cover all breast tissue within the defined perimeter. It should take five to eight minutes to examine each breast thoroughly. So you won't miss any tissue, do not lift your fingers from the breast.

You can use one of the following patterns:

1—vertical strip (Fig. 10)
2—wedge (Fig. 11)
3—circle (Fig. 12)

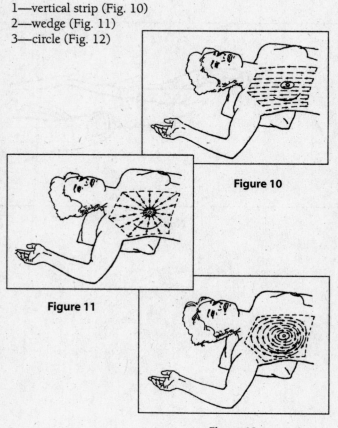

Figure 10

Figure 11

Figure 12

Vertical Strip Pattern:

To follow the vertical strip pattern, start palpating in dime-sized circles at the armpit and proceed downward until you reach the lower boundary. Then move a finger's width toward the middle and continue palpating back up the breast until you reach the upper boundary. Once again, move a finger's width toward the middle and continue downward. Repeat this until you have covered all the breast tissue. Make at least six strips before the nipple and four strips after the nipple. Be sure that one of the strips goes over the nipple so you can carefully palpate the nipple area. This search pattern is similar to mowing the lawn. You may need between 10 and 16 strips for each breast.

Wedge Pattern:

To carry out the wedge pattern, imagine your breast divided like the spokes of a wheel. Examine each segment individually, moving from the outside boundary toward the nipple. Slide fingers back to the boundary, move over a finger's width and repeat this until you have covered all the breast tissue. You may need between 10 and 16 segments for each breast.

Circle Pattern:

For the circle pattern, imagine the breast as the face of a clock. Start at 12 o'clock and palpate along the boundary of each circle until you return to your starting point. Then move down a finger's width and continue palpating in ever smaller circles until you reach the nipple. Be sure to palpate the nipple area carefully. Depending on the size of your breast, you may need 8 to 10 circles for each breast.

Nipple Discharge

Gently squeeze each nipple to check for discharge (Fig. 13).

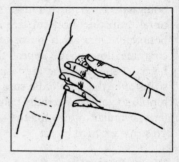

Figure 13

Axillary Examination

Examine the breast tissue that extends into the armpit while your arm is relaxed at your side (Fig. 14).

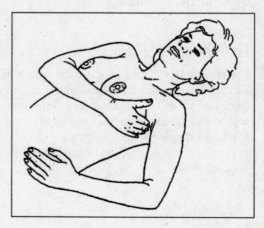

Figure 14

PRACTICE WITH FEEDBACK

It is important that you perform the breast self-exam while your instructor watches to be sure you are doing it correctly (Fig. 15). It may take some time before you feel confident in your skill. If you do not feel competent after several months, seek further instruction.

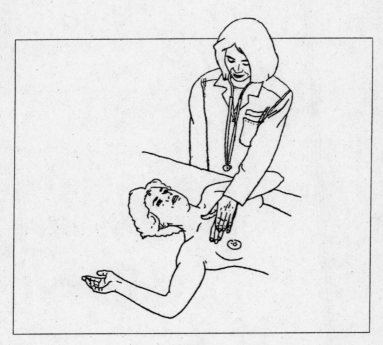

Figure 15

Chapter 14

Creating a Ten-Step Healing Plan

In business, we learn the importance of creating a plan and making a commitment to succeed. Within the plan, we define a vision, and create realistic goals that enable us to measure our accomplishments. It is our plan that keeps us focused and allows us to make the decisions that are best for our growth. Without a plan or a strategy for success, we risk losing the opportunity to reach our potential.

To ensure success in healing requires a similar plan. In the event that one is diagnosed with breast cancer or any other life-threatening disease, I feel it is essential to create an environment that allows healing to take place. This concept is based on the success of my own healing. My plan helped me stay focused and feel in control, particularly when many things seemed out of control.

Shortly after the word got out, I started receiving many calls, cards, and bouquets of flowers. At first, I was touched by all of the thoughtfulness. I soon discovered, however, that my energy was being directed toward reassuring everyone that I was fine. The overall perception I found myself up against was that cancer was the image of death. I started to feel exhausted by all of the sympathy I was receiving. So I asked John to read all of the cards, accept the flowers, and take the phone calls. I asked that he tell me about the individuals who were thinking of me without getting into specifics. It was most helpful to pull myself out of this picture and focus my attention on what I needed to do. I could still acknowledge each gesture with gratitude without feeling emotionally drained.

Unfortunately, most people know someone who has died from some form of cancer. I felt that this outcome was clearly not going to be the case with me. Although it's a natural response for an individual to remember someone who died, it is most definitely *not* comforting to hear about it when you are planning to live! In other words, it is best to focus on *being with the individual* rather than on the disease and what happened as a result.

Here are ten steps to help you create a healing plan. This structure can help you maintain your focus throughout your process.

Step 1: Vision.

Have a vision of what you will look and feel like once you are completely healed. This vision will help you create immediately what you desire. It is normal to experience changes in your attitude and behavior as a result of envisioning your life filled with joy and satisfaction. Ask yourself: What do I want my life to look like? What gives me joy? What do I need to do to create what I desire in my life? Picture yourself in the future, living your life exactly the way you want it to be. Create in your mind's eye the life you've always dreamed of. This places an invisible hook into what you want. Your vision needs to be very clear and attainable.

As I envisioned my future, I realized that my highest priority was to make this time *my* time, with nothing else competing with it. I began to make lists of questions to ask doctors. The real test for any doctor I chose to work with was the ability to answer all of my questions with a positive and open attitude. Since this was *my* time, my outlook was that I was hiring them to be active partners in my health and well-being. I was not interested in anything less.

My vision of the big picture allowed me to create goals that assisted immensely with my daily process of healing. Through meditation, I began to visualize not only my relationship with doctors, but the treatment room where I would be receiving chemotherapy, as well as the ultimate results of my surgeries. Each vision and goal solidified my plan, giving me great strength and fantastic results.

I also visualized a healing circle with two types of people: some who would assist me with my physical healing, and others who would assist me with my emotional healing. I then took the steps to actually create an amazingly powerful support team that consisted of truly wonderful people: Dr. John West, an outstanding surgeon; Dr. Brian Kent, my incredible plastic surgeon; Jean Sedbrook, an exceptional breast cancer survivor; Dr. John Glasby, a most understanding oncologist; Dr. Dennis Gowens, a special and gifted psychologist; Dr. John Rodino, a knowledgeable biochemist; Dr. David Chen, a loving acupuncturist; and Dr. Mark Campbell, an inspiring and thoughtful chiropractor. These angels went beyond the call of duty and made a significant difference in my life. May they each be blessed a thousandfold with what they individually gave to me.

This time became magical in its own way, as all the right people came together for the sole purpose of helping me heal. This is what the divine feminine spirit looks like. I was tremendously honored by each individual in my circle.

And *everything* that I envisioned manifested into reality.

See your healing as a clear vision and you
will experience an expansion of yourself.

Step 2: Involve your loved ones.

Since breast cancer is such a personal issue, it is most important to involve your mate in your process of healing. There is no greater support than that which can be found in a beloved. Women often underestimate the power that underlies the love of a man. A man can be as vulnerable at this time as his partner who is going through this process. Although many men may not express their feelings in the same way women do, they do experience many of the same emotions, including enormous anxiety and fear of the unknown. It is up to us to acknowledge and honor their feelings by bringing them in as an integral part of our healing. By shutting them out we not only do them a disservice, but we do ourselves a disservice as well. This is an opportunity for real love to flourish between partners. It is also an opportunity to heal more than breast cancer. You can create closure in a particular area of your life and create a new beginning with your mate. Adversity can change your life and your mate's for the better if you open yourself up to the possibilities.

In speaking with many breast cancer survivors, I have found that men who truly love us do not love us less because we are sick. They love us more during our time of healing, because they fear losing us. They cherish us completely, whether we have two breasts or not. A man who loves you will in fact be more concerned about your happiness and your life than the possibility of your losing a breast. Often, what hurts a man most is when his partner does not allow him in, for fear that he will not love her as much as he did before. Opening yourself up to him will give you an opportunity to love yourself.

For me, involving John was truly a blessing. His love and support allowed me the space I needed to heal spiritually, emotionally, and physically. Sharing this process with him allowed me to honor both of us. We supported each other with open communication and worked as a team. He came with me to every doctor's appointment and was the first person I woke up to see after each surgery. He was the one waiting anxiously yet patiently in the waiting room. He was the one who sat with me during my chemotherapy sessions. At times when no one else could possibly understand my reason for celebrating life, he was there.

I also involved my son's preschool teachers because I felt it was important that I provide a healthy environment for him and his sister. I wanted to be able to explain to my son Christopher—who was only four at the time—what was happening and what was going to happen, so that he would not feel as anxious or left out. I believed it was better to include him than to pretend that nothing was going on. At the suggestion of one of his teachers, Christopher created a special hug that he would give me when I was recovering from surgery. It warms my heart every time I think of this very special time. As a result, my healing did not interfere with our physical bonding. In fact, it made it all the more special.

When we open our hearts to those who love us, we acknowledge and bless their love. It frees us and lifts our spirit.

Step 3: Trust your instincts in choosing the right doctors for you.

Choosing the right doctors can at times seem difficult—particularly if you have a specific health plan (such as an HMO, for example). Your instincts can guide you in choosing what feels right for you. I believe that a woman's instincts are heightened when she is facing a life-or-death situation. There is no question in my mind that this is when our inner power has an opportunity to shine, perhaps like never before.

I felt very blessed at having found both Dr. West and Dr. Kent and bringing them onto my team as healing partners. It wasn't until I needed to speak to an oncologist that I realized the importance of interviewing doctors. Let me explain. Since in my case the cancer was found in its earliest stage, there was a question as to whether or not I needed chemotherapy. At first, I was referred to an oncologist who was covered by my health plan. Within minutes of my meeting him I knew this was not the man who would help me get better. When I asked about the need for further treatment, he told me how he had signed death certificates for many women who had been younger than I was. Needless to say, his words and his entire manner were very discouraging. My meeting with "Dr. Gloom" lasted less than ten minutes, and I walked out with tears in my eyes. I couldn't tell you which made me more sad: that women in their twenties were dying of breast cancer or that he did not convey a picture of life for me.

In a strange way, however, I will always be grateful to this man because the experience empowered me to identify what my standards were for choosing an oncologist. Since my insurance company agreed to pay for a second opinion, I decided to interview several doctors before hiring one. I felt it was necessary to have a preliminary meeting with each doctor to establish not only credibility, but also attitude and bedside manner. I had no intention of spending my insurance company's money on someone who potentially did not fit the bill.

In the medical world, it seemed quite out of the ordinary to request brief meetings with doctors to interview them. Yet, I usually meet with my mechanic before allowing him to work on my car! So it seemed perfectly logical to me. It was sort of strange to request an initial meeting, and insist on not giving any insurance information. I certainly had no intention of making things difficult. I just knew what I wanted, and I was not willing to settle for anything less.

My next meeting was with a female oncologist who had been highly recommended because she, too, had had breast cancer. While sitting with her, I realized that she had some personal issues regarding her healing that were not complete. Although she seemed sweet, I felt I needed someone who would view my case with fresh and inspiring eyes.

I was celebrating the fact that I caught this early. It was clear to me that I needed to stay focused on that reality alone. After reading *The Breast Book* by Dr. Susan Love, I decided to call her office in Los Angeles for a referral. Her staff in turn referred me to Dr. John Glasby. Within minutes of meeting him, I knew this was the man. His jovial personality and welcoming humor confirmed my instincts. In looking at my case, he felt it was a good idea to go ahead with the chemotherapy treatments based on the fact that the cancer was aggressive. I was grateful to get a straight answer even though I would have preferred a different one at the time.

He took John and me on a tour of the facility and

the treatment room. To my astonishment, the rooms were precisely what I had envisioned—down to the color of the furnishings and decor. I knew I was exactly where I needed to be. The treatment room was spacious, with floor-to-ceiling glass, and overlooked a garden that was also a sitting area. The chairs were exceptionally comfortable and the staff seemed friendly. My heart was happy with my decision.

The only challenge left was to get the insurance company's agreement to pay for services rendered by a doctor outside of my plan. John and I committed ourselves to do whatever we needed to in order to have Dr. Glasby as my oncologist. Through the advice of Managed Care, I was told that I needed to call Dr. Gloom and have him refer me to Dr. Glasby. This was an uncomfortable call, since I had to tell him why I had decided not to work with him. He graciously honored my request. (I must add that many women since then have unknowingly shared many success stories about this doctor. Although my initial encounter with him was discouraging, I may have caught him on a day when he lost a patient. I will never know. Nevertheless, I'm grateful for our meeting because it led me to stretch myself and become very clear about my healing.)

After three long days on the phone with various decision makers, we were granted our wish. Without a doubt, it was definitely worth it all!

Trust in your inner guidance,
for within it lies a multitude of gifts.

Step 4: Set your goals according to your vision.

One of the most important goals that I set for myself was to see the reflection of my body in a mirror in years to come and not be reminded that I had cancer. It was important to me that I come away with no emotional or cosmetic scars. Along with this goal came a strong commitment to communicate my specific needs with my surgeons. By this time, several women had come forth to kindly show me their cosmetic results. I was at times amazed at the length and size of some of the scars.

My tremendous anxiety about this motivated me to call Dr. West (on an urgent basis) at 6:00 A.M. on the Saturday prior to my scheduled bilateral surgery. My voice trembled as I requested he make the smallest incisions possible. He stated that he had no idea that this meant so much to me, and assured me that he would do everything in his power to comply with my wishes. With that, he went on to say that he would order special equipment for the operating room.

This was monumental, as it relieved me of my

anxiety. In fact, not only were the incisions the smallest he had ever made for a bilateral mastectomy, they represented a new possibility for other women. Shortly after surgery, Dr. West came by wearing the most contagious smile I'd ever seen. He said, "You've taught an old dog a new trick!" He was most pleased with his work, which made it easy for Dr. Kent to complete the reconstruction.

As a result, I have no visible scars, even though I have been completely "rebuilt." After four surgeries, including skin grafts and final tattooing, I consider it miraculous to have such results.

In addition, I requested that Dr. Kent inject collagen in my nipples for a little more fullness. At first he hesitated, because he didn't think it was necessary. He had never done this procedure, but was interested in its possibility. Thanks to Dr. Bond, my primary physician who gave me the idea, it was a success.

Today, I am very happy with my results. I'm grateful to have worked with two of the most accommodating, talented, and skilled doctors in the field.

Without goals, I simply would not have set the boundaries for my healing. I would not have been as focused or committed to follow through with my heart's desire. Set your goals based on what you want for your emotional and physical well-being. It can be a very powerful experience for you, as well as for your doctors!

Every time that each of us strives for a little more of what our heart desires, we create a pathway for other women and doctors to do the same. We set the tone for new patterns, new beliefs, and a new reality.

Step 5: The importance of asking questions.

Although each of these steps is equally important, peacefulness revisits the soul when we receive the answers necessary for our healing. Having a vision in place keeps us entirely focused and motivated to get all of the answers we need. There is no such thing as a right or wrong question to ask. Gathering information can seem effortless when you have a vision and a goal. The questions just seem to pour out, one after another. For example, without the vision of not being scarred, I wouldn't have thought to request that Dr. West make smaller incisions.

Allow the information to unfold. It is in your best interest, however, to take a good look at what's being offered as information. There were times in my process when someone else's reality was not mine to share, and this was OK. Remember, when it comes to healing, *all* things are possible. Let your heart be your guide.

Before each doctor's appointment, I found it

very helpful to write all of my questions down in the form of a list. I also meditated and envisioned receiving all of the answers I needed at the given time. Since clarity was at the top of my priority list, I was confident that I would make the decisions that were right for me, based on the information I received. This also created the space where regrets were not a possibility.

> *Knowledge is the mother of clarity and*
> *inner power. Without it we are overcome*
> *with fear and all of the "what-if's."*

Step 6: Attitude is the key!

It never ceases to amaze me to see the strength exuding from women who have been healed from and by breast cancer. Many of us experience it as a shot in the arm: permission to go and really *live* life. It is this enormously liberating permission that ignites our overall attitude about fully living our lives, and fulfilling our needs, wants, and desires.

Although having to heal from a serious illness is not something I wish on anyone, it does propel drastic change. There's a sense of expansion that takes place within the self. There's a sense of freedom that arrives with a new lease on life.

I believe it is vital to step into the space of *already being healed* while one is going through the various steps of the process. This establishes two things: it creates a positive message for the mind to deliver to the body; and it creates a forthright attitude, which is essential. I believe a healthy attitude is a determining factor in healing a disease.

If all breast cancer survivors were asked to list the ways this disease has led to healing in their lives, I know what their lists would look like. In fact, I know many women who wouldn't trade their experience for anything in the world because they see it as a blessing that led to personal transformation.

Here are just a few ways that this disease healed and enhanced my life:

+ The entire quality of my life has been enhanced through the discovery and awareness of the ten commonalities of women who got breast cancer (discussed in Chapter 1). I no longer live within the confines of those old patterns and beliefs.
+ I am now clear about what's important to me, and it reflects in all of my relationships. My understanding of this disease has broadened my awareness of people and life. I no longer come from judgment, only compassion.

✦ I have given myself no other choice but to live in my joy and to honor myself as a child of God. Herein lies the commitment to teach this to my children.

✦ I take better care of my body by not skipping meals and by eating high-quality foods. I remember to take my vitamins!

✦ I no longer take things for granted; I have a greater appreciation for the little things in life. Taking time to smell the roses is a natural occurrence for me.

✦ I now take time to recognize the individuals who have and continue to make a difference in my life. Sending flowers to each surgeon just a few hours before my surgeries seems so small in comparison to what they gave me.

✦ My healing taught me to receive willingly and lovingly. This alone has brought me to great heights. As a result, I now live a balanced life.

✦ Thanks to this experience, I have discovered a deeper sense of self, and strength and power I never knew I possessed. I have reclaimed my own divinity.

✦ I have found infinite passion for writing
   books, a gift to myself and to those who
   wish to receive it.
✦ At my very core now resides a feeling of
   deep gratitude. I thank God for all of the
   healing that has occurred in my life as a
   result of what some call "adversity."
   These changes have elevated me to a
   place of contentment and completion.
✦ Realigning with the divine feminine
   spirit was the greatest gift of all.

I encourage you to look at your own healing
journey and define the gifts it offers you.

You choose an attitude, just as you choose
what you are going to wear each day.
Know that your choices mirror your attitude.

Step 7: Establish a nutritional program for yourself.

There is no question in my mind that diet and
nutrition play an enormous role in the prevention
and the healing of breast cancer and other diseases.
Equally important are our core beliefs and atti-

tudes we hold in regard to food and its nutrients. The entire issue of diet and nutrition is the subject of much controversy. As a result, many are questioning what is truly good for us. Since every body and mind has different requirements, it is easy to understand why interpretations are numerous.

I believe that as women, many of us are so concerned with our weight and what society considers to be a "beautiful body" that we often unconsciously deprive our bodies of the proper nutrients. The simple joy of eating is compromised by the illusion of what advertisers tell us is "real beauty." The message we often give ourselves is that we are not good enough, and we feel guilty about the foods we eat. We have unconsciously bought into these beliefs. We make ourselves wrong for not weighing less, for not having the so-called "perfect body." This contributes to low self-esteem in women and the ten commonalities discussed in Chapter 1.

What's perhaps most interesting about a cancer diagnosis is that it propels us to define the real issue, which is saving our own life. Weight and the so-called perfect body are not the priority at hand. Finding the right foods to nourish our individual bodies and help us heal usually becomes a higher priority. Oddly enough, we suddenly give ourselves permission to eat what we choose, *without* the guilt. It is at this time that many of us open up to learning new information about the value of nutrition. I believe that the information we seek is precisely what we need in order to change our eating habits and our associations with food. Food becomes associated with good health instead of whether our body is perfect.

Our openness to learning and trusting in what we discover brings forth transformation. Here's one example. Given the fact that I was going to have chemotherapy, I began to prepare myself for the possibility of losing my hair. When I shared this with my hairstylist, Elaine, she insisted that I speak to a biochemist, Dr. John Rodino, and passionately described the success her granddaughter had experienced under his care. Not only had this little girl beautifully recovered from a life-threatening brain tumor, she had never lost a hair despite all of the treatments!

I believe that God places angels in our lives just when we need them, and Elaine was certainly one of those angels. Little did I know the many gifts that I would receive as a result of her suggestion.

Dr. Rodino received his first Ph.D. in chemistry with honors from Franklin University in 1962, his second Ph.D. in biochemistry with honors from the Oklahoma Institute of Technology in 1981, and is the author of a textbook titled *Interaction of Lipids and Protein*. He was part of a team and the work that was responsible for the development of several infant formulas, as well as the initial investigation into the development of lipoproteins and their biochemical functions in the human body. He also developed many pharmaceutical products and the majority of the prostaglandins (a group of enzymes that control organ and glandular functions) available today, including Betaplex, Hepagen, Ferex, Androgen, Femagen, Lipozyme, Pantoplex, and Triretic.

Meeting Dr. Rodino changed my entire view of diet and nutrition. After evaluating by blood work, which included more than fifty panels, he described my physical complaints with an astounding accuracy—better than I could! He also identified many of the foods that I enjoyed as directly contributing to my complaints. Sometimes his information seemed so far out of the norm, yet I was committed to his program because of the results I was achieving month after month.

Dr. Rodino believes that Americans in general have taken on many of the peasant diets and ways of eating that were brought here by immigrants. As a result, many cultures unconsciously brought in a high-carbohydrate diet. For example, the Italians brought us pasta and pizza; the Asians brought us rice and noodles; the Mexicans brought us rice, brown beans, and tortillas; and the Irish brought us potatoes—to name just a few. Although many would agree that these are delicious-tasting foods, Dr. Rodino believes they do not provide the body with the same level of nutrients found in high-quality proteins. The carbohydrates (better known as starches) are "fillers": they fill the belly but they don't truly feed the body. (Incidentally, the affluent people in each of the cultures mentioned are more likely to eat quality proteins such as seafood and various bird meats. The starch is not considered to be the main part of the meal.) Dr. Rodino adds, "Large quantities of starch in our diet can make us feel sluggish and lethargic, which leads to a *physical depression*."

If you've ever had a big pasta meal, you know it would be easy to take a nap right afterward! This is what physical depression feels like. Dr. Rodino also explains that when we feel emotionally depressed, it is common to crave starch since it literally feeds the depression. It tastes good, so it is temporarily soothing. Interestingly, these starches are also very fattening and turn into insulin in the body, which can lead to diabetes and high cholesterol levels.

Based on several decades of research and work with patients, Dr. Rodino believes that starch is the leading cause of premature death in this country. He has seen more people these days who are dieting and still gaining weight! Many people believe that a high-carbo diet is a low-fat diet; that these foods are not fattening, when they actually are. Dr. Rodino also believes that a country with poor eating habits is one that suffers in social and economic advancement due to the physical depression among its people.

This made sense to me, since both of my parents were born and raised in Italy during the war. My mother, talented and creative cook that she is, makes her own breads and pastas to this day. While I was growing up, food was considered a sacred and beautiful celebration of life. Although there was an abundance of seafood, meats, fruits, and vegetables, pasta was usually the main course.

Needless to say, I was committed to altering my diet and restricting my starch intake for the sake of getting well. This was no easy task. I had to reinvent my own cooking and get past the old Italian tradition of Sunday pasta dinners. However, it became easier as I noticed an increase in energy and an overall feeling of well-being, particularly during my months of chemotherapy. Restrictions included breads, pasta, cookies, cakes, corn, potatoes, pizza, alcohol, and cereal. My breakfast consisted of Genopro, a high-quality protein powder, blended with a banana and cranberry juice. Lunch was a salad with turkey, chicken, or shrimp, with lemon and extra virgin olive oil. Dinner usually consisted of any one of the major protein meats with an assortment of

vegetables and fruit for dessert. (Genopro is available through Kaylim Laboratories—see Resources.)

The issue of chemotherapy and its side effects
were explained as follows. By restricting uric acid–
releasing foods (such as milk, cheese, ice cream, red
meats, nuts, and brown beans) as well as foods high
in fats (such as mayonnaise, margarine, fried foods,
salad dressing, and alcohol), the liver would not
have to work as hard. This would allow Dr. Rodino
to use prostaglandins to help the liver repair itself,
thus reducing the likelihood of the liver becoming
inflamed, and helping the liver tolerate the toxic
effects of chemotherapy. The liver is then able to
continue its function of processing proteins and
forming enzymes required to keep the body functioning, while maintaining the reserves necessary
for chemotherapy. With the liver functioning normally, chemotherapy side effects—such as jaundice,
nausea, malaise, hair loss, and all the other problems that relate directly and indirectly to impaired
liver function—are dramatically reduced.

During my seven months of chemotherapy, I experienced energy and vitality unlike any before. If it
hadn't been for a simple mistake I made within the
diet itself, my recovery during the seven months
would have been flawless. I had undergone two
chemotherapy treatments when I decided to participate in a twenty-four-hour Easter Seals relay race. I

felt so healthy and vibrant that I ran two miles with intense pride. I felt happy to be alive and grateful for the opportunity to be part of such an event. Well, I felt the evening chill set in just as someone offered me a shot of peppermint schnapps. Not being much of a drinker, I took two small sips and went to join my children who were sleeping in the motor home.

The next morning I was greeted by small clumps of hair that had fallen out of my thick ponytail. After several agonizing hours of anxiety and intense uncertainty, I got through to Dr. Rodino. When I described what was happening, he calmly asked, "Stella, have you had any alcohol within the past forty-eight hours?" I gasped as I remembered that alcohol was one of the restrictions. When I told him precisely what and how much I drank, he said, "Stella, of all the alcohol and liquors, you chose one of the most lethal! When you combined those two sips of alcohol with the reserves you used up while running two miles, it caused your liver to become inflamed. The alcohol went straight to your clean liver and impaired its ability to process proteins, causing your hair to fall out. In fact, if you had had the whole shot, you would have lost *all* of your hair in about fifty minutes!" I could not believe that I had brought this on myself! I had completely forgotten about the alcohol. He reassured me that my hair would stop falling out. He adjusted my program just a bit and my hair loss stopped after a few weeks, precisely as he said it would.

(Dr. Rodino suggests that champagne is the cleanest form of alcohol to drink since it is low in sugar and phosphates. It is also free of starch in contrast to wine and beer.)

Fortunately, my hair loss wasn't noticeable to others, but it did have its effects on me emotionally. I had completely ruled out the possibility of hair loss after I committed myself to Dr. Rodino's diet and program. So, needless to say, I was shocked.

Yet from my mistake, a gift was received. I now am able to feel compassion for individuals who lose their hair, and for the many emotions that accompany such an ordeal. Without this experience, I would not have this understanding. It is easy to say, "Oh, it will grow back." Yet, it's not that easy when you're the one watching your hair fall out! It can be very traumatic, especially for women.

I believe that each of us knows within our hearts what works for us and what doesn't. You know a diet works for you when you feel empowered by it, not enslaved.

Bless the foods you eat, for as you bless them, you bless your body with your own healing power. Food is meant to be enjoyed

> *and cherished; not only does it nourish*
> *your body, the pure enjoyment feeds*
> *your mind and your spirit.*

Step 8: Fashion and self-image.

Given my background in fashion and self-image, I feel it is important to recognize that the way we dress helps us to maintain a positive outlook, especially during a stressful time. Enhancing our self-image helps us to feel a sense of control. It also serves as a diversion and directs our energy toward self-improvement and self-empowerment.

I strongly recommend taking time to clear out any clothing that no longer serves you by either giving it away or just removing it from your closet. Make every effort to avoid the "what-if's," because those are what keep us stuck. Wear only what you love and what makes you feel great. I see this as part of the cleansing and healing process. It is refreshing to go to your closet knowing that whatever you choose to wear, you'll feel confident about how you look. Make this a fun exercise by creating a list of needs for your next shopping trip.

More often than not, women tend to believe that the clothes in their closets don't fit their needs, and that they have "nothing to wear" (that they like). One of my greatest joys in my business as a wardrobe consultant was opening a closet full of clothes and creating endless possibilities. I once went to a woman's house to evaluate her wardrobe. She was convinced that she had a closet full of *boring* clothes and nothing to wear! Her style of dress included classic, conservative lines; and she had grown tired of this look.

After twenty minutes of sorting and evaluating, I asked her to bring out all her accessories, such as scarves, belts, and jewelry. She brought out some of the most beautiful pieces of costume jewelry I'd ever seen, which she had purchased all over the world. I immediately started combining these items with various dresses and separates hanging in her closet. Together we created over fifty new looks just by mixing and matching her clothes with this incredible jewelry that she hardly ever wore! In addition, we took pictures of each ensemble and created a small list of items she could purchase in the future. She was ecstatic with her new wardrobe, and we had a fabulous time creating it!

I share this with you because, as women, we are at our best when we are creating! We don't realize how exhausting it is to make things wrong for ourselves. This is harmful to the spirit; it stifles the very fiber of our being. So, if you are less than happy about your clothing or the way you look, let your creativity flow. Do your best to not use the money issue as an excuse, because a lot can be done with very little money. Most women have gold mines in their wardrobes and are not aware of it.

Some tips for shopping include:

1. Purchase only what you love and what makes you feel great.
2. Trust your instincts and do not purchase anything if there is *any* doubt. Your doubts will go home with you and haunt you every time you think about that purchase!
3. Shop for comfort as well as style.
4. Do your best to shop for items that coordinate with at least three other items in your wardrobe.
5. Avoid buying on impulse.
6. Cut out pictures from fashion magazines to have a clear idea of what you want.
7. Pay attention to which stores are having sales, and when. This knowledge allows you to budget for your needs.
8. Wear or bring with you the proper undergarments while selecting your new clothing.
9. Wear new undergarments to help you feel beautiful before you put anything

else on. I can't tell you how many women will spend hundreds of dollars on clothes and shoes while wearing their bras pinned together!

10. Purchase high-quality merchandise; it will reflect in the way it looks and feels to you. These items will most certainly last longer and they will wear beautifully cleaning after cleaning.

The way you dress expresses how you feel about yourself. If you are happy with the way you look, you will feel vibrant and happy. This can really come in handy on a day when the physical body is not feeling as well as we would like it to. For example, I found it helpful to wear something red on the days when I was feeling less than great. Wearing red, a vibrant color and one of my favorites, gave me energy and made me feel good. I paid close attention to this particularly on the days I would be receiving chemotherapy treatments. Selecting something to wear that filled my spirit helped me to stay focused on feeling good. It also created an environment where people would compliment me on how I looked instead of asking how I felt. I enjoyed hearing people say, "You look great!" This proved to be very beneficial, and took me away from all of the mind chatter.

I also found that purchasing new makeup during

this time was very helpful. A new shade of lipstick can easily and inexpensively brighten your face! Your face is the first thing people see when they look at you. Treat yourself to a facial and a make-over. It's fun to explore the suggestions a make-up consultant may have for you. Choose shades of colors that enhance your natural beauty and make you feel good.

Treat yourself to a teeth cleaning, and consider whitening your teeth. Your smile is your greatest asset.

Use this time of healing as a training ground to establish a new way of being—a time for honoring yourself and loving yourself.

> *Honoring yourself brings forth*
> *the effortless commitment to a*
> *healthy and positive self-image.*

Step 9: Record your accomplishments.

I cannot overemphasize the importance of writing your thoughts, feelings, desires, questions, answers, and accomplishments. This is an outstanding way to achieve clarity on many of the issues, particularly when so many decisions need to be made. My personal experience and the writings of my healing process resulted in the first draft for this book (over three hundred pages of writing, but then again, I love to write!).

My journal was part of my daily ritual; and I used it when I needed to release or clarify feelings. There were nights when I couldn't sleep and my journal was there to gently comfort me. Writing made me feel safe and peaceful when I grew restless and impatient.

I discovered a format that you may find effective in learning to trust yourself. Simply meditate for a few minutes, then write down a question and follow it with an answer. Continue this process, answering all of the questions that come up in your mind. This is an amazing method that brings peace of mind as you realize that you truly have the answers to all of the questions within you. I usually like to end my day with this simple exercise since it helps me release any thoughts or concerns. It helps me sleep soundly and wake up eager to start a new day. I have found that it is easy to stay focused and to know that I can tap into that space at any time. It has assisted me in embracing my relationship with myself, also known as my spirituality.

I encourage you to find just a few minutes in your day to reflect on your experiences. Discover your own methods of staying true to yourself through writing.

Keeping a journal of your accomplishments
enhances your ability to recognize
just how powerful you truly are.

Step 10: Meditate and pray; be grateful.

Meditation and prayer are the keys to balance in one's life. This balance is, in my opinion, the core expression *of* the human spirit and *for* the human spirit. When we meditate, we allow ourselves to receive that which we need to hear, and that which otherwise may not have entered our consciousness. I believe that when we meditate we *receive* information allowed to us only in that sacred space. In prayer, we speak and *give* our thoughts, our wishes, our gratitude, and our blessings. This combination creates a harmonious dance that encompasses the spirit, the mind, and the body. It is within this circular inner dance that all healing takes place. It is whole. It is pure and it is love. Many of us relate to this feeling as feeling the presence of God. We feel so loved. We experience the many miracles that manifest as a result of trusting and believing.

This conscious declaration is the spiritual dance that is created *within the self*, as the divine feminine and the divine masculine come together for the highest good of all concerned. In this space of meditation and prayer, there is no guilt or self-criticism, just unconditional self-love. We declare healing as a natural part of life!

> *Healing in the world begins*
> *with honoring oneself.*

A WOMAN'S PRAYER

Thank you, Lord,
For teaching me to honor myself.
For in doing so, I honor not only those who are
    close to me,
But all of your creation.
And thank you, Lord,
For helping me find the perfect balance I seek
    in all things,
For in doing so, the story of my life unfolds
    easily and naturally,
Creating an inner harmony that is contagious
    to everyone I meet.
And Lord, thank you, too,
For those things I sometimes take for granted,
Like family and friends,
Like laughter and talent and tears,

Like music and movies and dancing and years . . .
Help me, Lord, to use these and all the wonderful
    gifts you've given me to better myself.
For in doing so, my heart will finally be healed.
Because it is only in honoring myself,
That I can truly begin to honor others,
And to learn to live more fully
The joy of honoring You.

—IN HONOR OF ALL WOMEN
BY SUE PARKER

Chapter 15 How to Support Someone Who Is Recovering from Breast Cancer

The best way to support someone who is recovering from breast cancer or any life-threatening disease is to support the spirit within the person. Allowing someone the space to heal in the way *she* wants to heal can be perhaps the greatest challenge.

In one case, I worked with Salina (fictitious name), a woman who was very angry with her sister, who had recently been diagnosed with breast cancer. She simply could not understand why her own sister would not take her calls, why she wouldn't get a second opinion, and why she wasn't taking a more aggressive approach to healing. In the short time I spent with Salina, I could see that her focus was on the well-being of her nieces and nephews, while blaming her sister for being selfish by not taking a more aggressive approach. This was her sister's second bout with cancer and I gathered that her sister was very tired of having to listen to and take care of everyone else's needs. I also sensed that she was experiencing a lot of guilt about pulling away from everyone. Although Salina loved her sister very much, she could help her greatly by giving her the space to do what *she* needed to do to get well, without dwelling on the negative possibility of leaving her children behind.

This situation is extremely difficult for *any* mother who is struggling to stay alive. It's easy for the mother to make herself feel wrong for being selfish at a time when she desperately needs to be. If Salina and her family could support this woman's spirit, it would lighten the load of having to deal with everyone else's expectations. The woman would find it easier to be true to herself, which is what healing is all about.

I certainly understood Salina's desire to help, and didn't judge her for her feelings. In fact, I empathized with her and gave her some insight that I hoped would help her release some of her fear of losing her sister. In this case, fear disguised itself as anger. I believe that once Salina chooses to acknowledge her fear, she will be able to release the need to control her sister's healing process, and reestablish their lines of communication. Identifying the fact that she doesn't want to lose her sister opens her heart to her truth, and opens herself up to *unconditionally* loving her sister. We all know that love is what heals, especially when it is unconditional.

Lighten the load of all the "shoulds," "woulds," and "coulds" for the individual and do your very best to stay in the moment. It's the little things that make all the difference in the world. Do your best to not mention anyone else's case unless it is a positive and uplifting account. Invest in some inspirational books that focus on love and healing. Excellent choices are *Chicken Soup for the Surviving Soul*, by Jack Canfield, Mark Victor Hansen, Patty Aubery, and Nancy Mitchell, R.N.; and *Chicken Soup for the Woman's Soul*, by Jack Canfield, Mark Victor Hansen, Marci Shimoff, and Jennifer Hawthorne. They are full of wonderful and inspirational true stories about real people. I highly recommend reading these books together, and sharing your thoughts and feelings.

The beauty of healing is that we do not have to be sick to experience the healing that takes place in the heart. I believe that many people experience some form of healing when they are around someone who is recovering from cancer or any life-threatening disease.

One of the nicest things you can do for someone is to plan future events with them. This helps elevate their spirit and places energy on the possibility of prolonging one's life. Many people in this situation go on to experience long, fulfilling lives, quite the opposite of what their doctors viewed as "reality." I believe much of this can be attributed to the spirit of the individual and how strong that spirit is. I feel that too many doctors rush to give an "expiration date" to individuals, automatically placing energy in a negative place. In my opinion, no one should ever be given an expiration date. In many cases, what doctors view as reality is based on numbers and statistics that completely overlook the power of the individual spirit. The spirit, on the other hand, *cannot* be measured, but is where healing begins. This is why, very often, what a doctor may view as reality is not what the *patient* views as reality! The decision to live is in the hands of the individual and his or her God. In any case, one can certainly plan events that are joyful and filled with celebration. There are always reasons to celebrate life!

Whenever possible, lighten the load of any responsibilities of those who are recovering from an illness. Offer to bring over a meal or drive them to their treatments. I strongly suggest creating a pact or an agreement, based on truth and open communication, so the individual feels comfortable about asking for and receiving what is needed. I recently heard about a woman who had asked each of her friends to spend a week with her during her chemotherapy treatments. What a great idea! This woman was setting the stage for a successful recovery and opening herself up to receive.

A wonderful way to offer support is to show your heartfelt affection with a hug. There is a type of hug that has proven to be extremely effective; it's called a "heart-to-heart hug." In a seminar I attended, Mark Victor Hansen described it as follows: Hugging an individual to the right, where the left side of your cheek touches the left side of the person's cheek, allows both hearts to meet. He demonstrated that when muscle-tested, the individuals actually felt stronger. He also encouraged us to kneel when we hug children, so that we meet them on their level, for the sole purpose of bringing our hearts together and helping them feel stronger.

Hugs are a vital and wonderful way of making someone feel special. Use the coupon on the following page to brighten someone's day!

Last but not least, be true to yourself. Don't hide your feelings of the heart. If necessary, allow tears to flow. Otherwise, you may find yourself exhausted—which can lead to resentment. Look for the gifts in every situation.

A sense of humor is refreshing, and laughter really is the best medicine! I'll never forget my last chemotherapy treatment. After signing in, I walked over to sit next to John. Then I noticed my best friend, Linda, dressed up like a streetwalker, with a wig and the whole nine yards, handing him a bottle of champagne! The look on his face made me laugh *so* hard, because he didn't recognize her at all! It still makes me laugh when I think of that day!

HUG COUPON

*Hugs are fat-free,
sugar-free, and
require no batteries.
Hugs reduce blood pressure,
body temperature,
and heart rate, and
help relieve pain
and depression.
Redeem this coupon
at your nearest
participating human being.
Returns cheerfully accepted.*
—AUTHOR UNKNOWN

Chapter 16 Lymphedema Awareness

The following is a chapter excerpted from a forthcoming book by JoAnn Rovig written for patients about lymphedema and self-care techniques. Ms. Rovig is an expert in the field. Her professional credentials include the following: certified therapist in Manual Lymph Drainage (MLD), Dr. Vodder School, Walchsee, Austria, August 1992; certified therapist in Complex Physical Therapy (CPT), University of Adelaide, Australia (Dr. John Casley-Smith), February 1994; certified therapist in Complete Decongestive Physiotherapy (CDP) Földi Technique.

JoAnn was the first therapist in North America to be certified in all three internationally recognized lymphedema treatment modalities, and opened the first lymphedema clinic in the Northwest in 1991. She has developed self-care programs that allow patients to control their condition after therapy, and she has produced two self-care videos. It is my hope that this information will inspire you, as it has me, to focus on self-care and nurturing.

I have learned from personal experience that cancer can be a new beginning. A life-threatening illness propels you to confront your own mortality with an immediacy that crowds out most of what you previously thought was important.

My interest in massage therapy and the healing arts began as the result of a degenerative spinal condition and fibromyalgia which made work impossible. After experiencing pain relief from a series of massage treatments, I decided to pursue the study of this transformative therapy. In 1988, just a month short of graduation, I was diagnosed with breast cancer. Opting for conservative treatment, I underwent a lumpectomy and radiation therapy. I learned from my studies that lymph node removal put me at risk for developing lymphedema (an abnormal swelling of the arm and/or hand); this knowledge provided a focus for my body therapy work.

It became clear immediately after opening my practice that lymphedema patients were frightened and isolated because they neither understood their condition, nor were receiving effective help. Lymphedema training, originally begun as a quest to help myself, quickly became a passion to bring this knowledge to others. Being able to offer lymphedema patients new hope and watch them regain control of their lives has been a thrill I can't describe, and it has also been an integral part of my own healing process.

It's not unusual for a patient to experience a 30 percent reduction in swelling after five days of in-clinic treatment. After learning self-help techniques and working on themselves for an additional two weeks at home, patients can often double that percentage. These kinds of success stories are what kindled my self-help crusade, which has now expanded to lectures, outreach programs, and self-care videos.

The following summary of what is known about lymphedema will dispel some of the anxiety you may have about developing lymphedema. It will give you the necessary information in advance of any complications that may develop after surgery. It is my hope that it will empower you to make informed decisions and manage your own recovery at a level that would not otherwise be possible. The body has its own healing and regenerative powers. This information illustrates how that process can be supported in noninvasive ways.

What Is the Lymphatic System?

Almost everyone has a basic understanding of the cardiovascular system and how it works: the heart pumps oxygenated blood through arteries until it reaches the tissue spaces through a network of arterial capillaries. After nutrient and waste exchange, deoxygenated blood is returned to the heart through the venous system. The lymphatic system is a secondary circulatory system that works in tandem with the cardiovascular system but has different functions. Lymph consists of plasma and other substances that form in tissue spaces throughout the body. It continually eliminates waste and toxic substances through a delicate network of tiny vessels and nodes throughout the body. Most tissue fluids are absorbed into the venous capillaries. The remainder, which often contains proteins and particles too large to be absorbed by the venous capillaries, is picked up by lymph vessels and filtered through lymph nodes before being returned to the bloodstream. The lymphatic system also plays an important role in immune function.

A normal lymphatic system is capable of removing ten times more fluid from the tissue than is necessary for normal metabolism. Edema is any swelling caused by excess fluid buildup in the tissues. This is normally experienced with localized infections, or in the case of an injury (such as a sprained ankle), there may be initial swelling (traumatic edema) which generally subsides within a few days. When there is serious damage to the lymphatic system (surgery or radiation), transport capacity is reduced or lost. Whether or not lymphedema develops depends on individual differences in the body's ability to compensate, which can include factors such as a person's general health, weight, lifestyle, and the extent of damage to the lymphatic channels. There is also a condition called primary lymphedema in which the lymphatic system fails because of a congenital weakness. In primary or secondary lymphedema, the swelling is chronic, does not subside, and gets progressively worse if not properly treated, causing permanent tissue changes and other serious complications.

Until recently, the importance of an intact, fully functional lymph system was not completely appreciated. Lymph tissues such as tonsils and adenoids were often hastily removed because they swelled during infections. It was not realized that these lymph nodes played an important role in fighting infection. With cancer surgery the first consideration is saving a life and often lymph node removal and/or radiation is mandatory. The possibility of developing lymphedema is of secondary concern. However, there is new technology emerging called "sentinel node mapping," which may allow women who are node-negative to avoid axillary dissection. As explained by Dr. Benjamin O. Anderson, assistant professor of surgical oncology at the University of Washington:

> *Cancer spreads from the tumor in the breast*
> *by lymphatic flow to the lymph node basin*
> *under the arm. Dye and/or radioactive tracer*

is injected into the breast at the site of the tumor to allow the breast surgery team to identify the first "downstream" node or few nodes from the cancerous breast tumor. That node is then removed and analyzed. If this technique proves reliable, as it has in melanoma, then some women who do not have cancerous spread to the sentinel node may be able to forgo removal of the remaining nodes, thereby avoiding the risk of subsequent lymphedema.

Those who have been through cancer treatment are most concerned about metastases, but many are also left with a damaged lymphatic system in the area where they had surgery and radiation. It is difficult to estimate postsurgical risk factors. One day the system becomes overwhelmed, shuts down, and swelling becomes noticeable. This can happen anywhere from several weeks to several years after surgery. It can be triggered by injury, infection, overexertion, and the normal aging process as skin loses elasticity and circulation slows down. It's even possible for air travel to trigger a lymphedema episode because the decrease in cabin pressure at altitude also decreases tissue pressure, which affects lymph flow.

Lymphedema Treatment—A Brief History

Until recently, the best that North American medicine has been able to offer lymphedema patients is compressive pump therapy as an attempt to reduce swelling. Unfortunately, this technique has very limited success and may do more damage to the affected limb because the excess fluid has no way to be shunted from the limb to functional lymph pathways. Patients are often told that "Nothing can be done" or "You will just have to live with it." Thanks to a number of very dedicated scientists in the field of lymphology, lymphedema no longer needs to be a debilitating condition.

In the 1930s, a Danish physiotherapist, Dr. Emil Vodder, discovered that lymph flow could be accelerated and redirected around damaged lymph vessels to alternate pathways. Modern lymphedema therapy takes advantage of the fact that there are many superficial lymph channels just beneath the surface of the skin. Therapists who are trained to treat lymphedema learn the pathways of lymph flow and employ very specific sequences of massage-like strokes that gently stretch the skin and route lymph fluid to functional channels. This procedure is called "Manual Lymph Drainage,"® and all of the hands-on lymphedema therapy techniques being used throughout the world today are based on its principles. The Vodder School in Austria still exists and graduates highly skilled therapists. It has taken years to get this information to North America, partly because the courses were not taught in English until the mid-1980s. There is still considerable skepticism in North America that such a gentle, seemingly simple technique could produce such profound results.

By 1960, Drs. Michael and Ethel Földi had combined the Vodder lymph drainage principles with compression bandaging, exercise, and skin care, calling their treatment "Complete Decongestive Physiotherapy." In 1980 they began treating lymphedema patients in their 140-bed treatment center near Freiburg, Germany. Their clinic has treated over 20,000 lymphedema patients and trained 8,000 therapists from all over the world.

In 1959, Dr. John Casley-Smith, a Rhodes scholar from Australia, began his research in lymphology, and in 1983 he and Dr. Michael Földi published their findings in the book, *Lymphangiology*. Dr. Casley-Smith's wife, Judith, who has an M.A. in kinesiology, used this data, her knowledge of anatomy, and Vodder lymph drainage principles to develop a technique that could be easily taught to patients and their partners. Her work pioneered the self-help approach to lymphedema management.

The Importance of Bandaging

Compression bandaging is a critical step in the lymphedema treatment process. Bandages are applied immediately following treatment sessions to maintain adequate tissue pressure and prevent fluid from backing up into the extremity. These nonelastic (short-stretch) bandages are manufactured specifically for the treatment of lymphedema and are not the same as Ace wraps. They provide a counterpressure, or resistance, for the pumping action of the muscles. As muscle contractions push against the bandages, the lymph vessels are compressed, forcing fluid upward. Care must be taken to create a gradient pressure to prevent backflow.

As treatment progresses, the body "remodels" and lymphatic channels are rerouted. Swelling is reduced and once it stabilizes, less maintenance is required. Compression support garments can then be substituted for daytime bandages. Lymphedema overstretches the skin and once excess fluid is removed, a support garment is needed until the loose skin remodels and normal tissue pressure is recovered. Eventually, elevating the limb at night and periodic daytime use of a compression garment may be all that is necessary.

Length of Treatment

The type and duration of lymphedema therapy required depends upon the severity of the condition. If the lymphedema has existed for a long time, the limb is grossly enlarged and tissue changes have taken place. Treatment by a professional is mandatory in these instances. If treatment begins in the early stages of lymphedema, it is easier to get the limb back to normal size. Patients can often be taught self-care methods so they can manage their condition at home after a short period of treatment and instruction. If you suspect that you have lymphedema, it is important to have an evaluation by a physician who understands the lymphatic system. Based on the doctor's assessment, you can then get a referral to a certified lymphedema therapist.

In addition to the physical and psychological changes caused by lymphedema, it's important to understand that certain complications are very serious and can be life-threatening, which is why it's necessary to be under a physician's care. Protein-rich lymph fluid is an ideal medium for bacterial growth and recurring infections. Skin problems can trigger an episode of lymphedema in individuals at risk, so meticulous skin hygiene is essential. Care must be taken to guard against any irritant or break in the skin that would allow entry of a pathogen: insect bites, pet scratches, rose thorns, even sunburn. Optimal functioning of the lymphatic system can be enhanced by exercise and a healthy, low-sodium diet.

Success rates in controlling lymphedema are directly related to the initial commitment of time and energy in decongestive therapy and self-care. Preventive care and early treatment will prevent more severe complications. Patients who are able to do self-care gain the satisfaction of knowing that they are helping to restore function to damaged lymphatic pathways with each self-massage stroke. Lymphedema is a condition that immediately and visibly responds to techniques that most patients can learn. A healthy lifestyle will also help sustain results.

Lymphedema Treatment and the Health Care System

Because of the current upheaval in the structure of health care delivery in North America and the scarcity of insurance funding, patients are being forced to take a more active role in their own healing process. There is major emphasis on preventive care and a healthier lifestyle. Although at times this seems unfair, it has a very positive aspect. We have a responsibility to learn the art of staying well. Because lymphedema is a chronic condition that requires ongoing attention and maintenance, the best way to keep it under control is for patients to learn to care for themselves once their condition has been stabilized. If they understand the lymphatic system and learn basic self-help massage and bandaging techniques, they will quickly discover that they can lead normal, independent lives without excessive dependency on medical professionals, and they may never require more expensive, invasive treatments. Through empowerment comes freedom.

No one needs a daily reminder of the trauma of cancer, and the medical community and insurance companies must realize that lymphedema can often be more difficult to cope with than cancer. Their understanding and participation in treating lymphedema is vital to broad spectrum cancer treatment.

Lymphedema and Your Future

The postoperative stage of cancer treatment is a time to nurture yourself: not to be angry about what has happened but to support the body and participate in your own recovery. It is reassuring to equip yourself with this new knowledge and gratifying to pass it along to others in need. You can become part of the advocacy that proves patients don't "have to live with lymphedema." Lymphedema, cancer, and any other serious illness can be viewed as opportunities. The process of recovery may permit you to reassess your personal priorities and carry on with your life path at a much deeper and more gratifying level than ever before.

For more information about lymphedema re-search, treatment, clinics, and self-help materials, contact the organizations listed in the resource guide [at the end of this book].

© 1997 BY JOANN ROVIG

I had my first bout with lymphedema a few years after my bilateral mastectomies. I specifically remember the swelling in my left hand and arm that was brought on by holding my daughter who was two and a half years old. It was during former President Richard Nixon's funeral that I held her for over two hours with my left arm while holding an umbrella with my right hand. The next day I awakened with a swollen, throbbing, and very painful left hand, fingers, and arm. I felt feverish and had flu-like symptoms. I did not know it at the time, but this was clearly an infection that I experienced, which lasted about a week. I simply thought I had the flu and attributed the pain in my arm to being sore from holding Arianna.

It wasn't until I experienced a second infection that I realized the excruciating pain in my arm was not normal. My arm felt as though it had been caught in a car door and was on fire. I could do nothing to relieve it. Dr. West immediately gave me a prescription for antibiotics, and the pain diminished within a few days. The swelling, however, still fluctuates and has not gone away completely.

I have noticed that salt intake and rapid changes in weather—particularly hot weather—increase the swelling. I have had two elastic sleeves custom-tailored to help manage the fluid buildup, but have not noticed any major changes.

After speaking with Saskia R. J. Thiadens, R.N., who is the president and founder of the nonprofit organization the National Lymphedema Network (NLN), and viewing JoAnn Rovig's video on self-care, I decided to contact JoAnn personally. For the first time I felt comfort in knowing that there was hope in not only addressing this condition, but in controlling it. Until this point, I experienced anxiety, uncertainty, and frustration due to the lack of information that was available. The language in regard to this condition seemed incredibly devastating and certainly unrealistic—that is, according to my standards. I simply found it unacceptable to limit myself in any way due to the swelling in my arm and hand. Needless to say, speaking to JoAnn was like a breath of fresh air.

Women are getting significant results through treatments and self-care in just a few days! I thought to myself: This is very exciting! So, after several conversations, I decided to fly to Seattle and go through the five-day program with JoAnn. As one of three individuals in the class, I began to notice a real difference in my fingers and hand within the first two days.

Unfortunately, due to an unexpected allergic reaction to shellfish just a couple of days before starting the program, I broke out in a skin rash. I had to stop my treatments because my skin was so irritated that I simply couldn't tolerate the bandages on my arm. At first I was disappointed, but JoAnn assured me that this was most likely a temporary setback, and that I could resume my self-care and self-massage at my leisure, once things settled down. However, the priority was to give my body a chance to heal completely from the reaction, and so we discontinued treatments. JoAnn's loving manner and encouraging words gently comforted me as I continued to attend the daily classes, focusing on specific information and exercises.

The goal for every person who enrolls in this program is to diminish the swelling and to have a normal-size arm and/or hand. One individual in the class experienced a 40 percent reduction in swelling in just three days, and a remarkable 73 percent in eleven days! I personally look forward to achieving my own results, confident that a great deal can be achieved with awareness and commitment to self.

JoAnn is truly an inspiration, as she continues with her commitment to self-care. What I love about her program is that it empowers us to take control, feel confident about our health, and gain independence through proper education. This is the gift that she offers, and it can make a tremendous difference in our lives! She offers us an opportunity to use the information so that we can get on with our lives without the limitation of lymphedema.

It's people like JoAnn Rovig and Saskia R. J. Thiadens, R.N.—who have completely devoted themselves to providing education, guidance, service, and most of all loving support—that are breaking ground in the world of lymphedema. In fact, in January of 1997, Saskia broke new ground by requesting Congresswoman Anna G. Eshoo to include as part of HR164 (a bill entitled the "Reconstructive Breast Surgery Benefits Act of 1997") a rider that would specifically address coverage of treatment for lymphedema. This is tremendously exciting! If passed, it will help many, many women. Saskia is truly a gem, and a gift to all who seek knowledge about this condition. I particularly appreciate her incredible healing energy and passion for helping people get support and proper care.

It was initially through Saskia that I was able to better educate myself on prevention of lymphedema. Saskia's Eighteen Steps to Prevention that follow are an important guide for any woman who has had a mastectomy, lumpectomy, or modified radical mastectomy in combination with axillary node dissection and/or radiation therapy. I believe that, had I been given this guide earlier, I probably would have prevented myself from having this condition. (Then again, I believe that everything happens for a reason. Perhaps it was so that I could share this information with you.)

EIGHTEEN STEPS TO PREVENTION
by Saskia R. J. Thiadens, R.N.

For the breast cancer patient who is at risk of lymphedema, and for the breast cancer patient who has developed lymphedema.

Who Is at Risk?

At risk is anyone who has had either a simple mastectomy, a lumpectomy, or a modified radical mastectomy in combination with axillary node dissection and, often, radiation therapy. Lymphedema can occur immediately after surgery, within a few months, a couple of years, or twenty years or more after cancer therapy. With proper education and care, lymphedema can be avoided or, if it develops, kept well under control.

The following instructions should be carefully reviewed before surgery and discussed with your physician or therapist.

1. Absolutely do not ignore any increase of swelling in your arm, hand, fingers, or chest wall, no matter how slight. *(If you notice ANY swelling, consult with your doctor immediately.)*

2. Never allow an injection or have blood drawn in the affected arm(s).

3. Have blood pressure checked in the unaffected arm.

4. Keep the edemic arm, or "at-risk" arm, spotlessly clean. Use lotion (Eucerin) after bathing. When drying it, be gentle but thorough. Make sure it is dry in any creases and between the fingers.

5. Avoid vigorous, repetitive movements against resistance with the affected arm (scrubbing, pushing, pulling).

6. Avoid heavy lifting with the affected arm. Never carry heavy handbags or bags with over-the-shoulder straps.

7. Do not wear tight jewelry or elastic bands around affected fingers or arm(s).

8. Avoid extreme temperature changes when bathing and washing dishes, and avoid saunas and hot tubs. Keep the arm protected from the sun.

9. Avoid any type of trauma (bruising, cuts,

sunburn, other burns, sports injuries, insect bites, cat scratches).

10. Wear gloves while doing housework, gardening, or any type of work that could result in even a minor injury.

11. When manicuring your nails, avoid cutting your cuticles. (*Let your manicurist know this is important to you.*)

12. Exercise is important, but consult with your therapist first. Do not overtire an arm at risk. If it starts to ache, lie down and elevate it. Recommended exercises: walking, swimming, light aerobics, bike riding, and specially designed ballet or yoga. (*Do not lift more than fifteen pounds.*)

13. When traveling by air, patients with lymphedema must wear a compression sleeve. Additional bandages may be required on a long flight.

14. Patients with large breasts should wear light breast prostheses (heavy prostheses may put too much pressure on the lymph nodes above the collarbone). Soft pads may need to be worn under the bra strap. Wear a well-fitted bra: not too tight and with no wire support.

15. Use an electric razor to remove hair from axilla (armpit). Maintain electric

         razor properly, replacing heads as needed.

16. Patients who have lymphedema should wear a well-fitted compression sleeve. See your therapist for follow-up at least every four to six months. If the sleeve is too loose, most likely your arm circumference has reduced or the sleeve is worn.

17. *Warning:* If you notice a rash, blistering, redness, increase in temperature, or fever, see your physician immediately. An inflammation or infection in the affected arm could be the beginning or worsening of lymphedema.

18. Maintain your ideal weight through a well-balanced, low-sodium diet. Avoid smoking and alcoholic beverages. Lymphedema is a high-protein edema, but eating less protein will not reduce the protein element in the lymph fluid. Rather, this will weaken the connective tissue and worsen the condition. The diet should contain protein that is easily digested, such as chicken, fish, or tofu.

The following discusses what many women who have lymphedema fear the most: an infection.

Lymphangitis (Infection)

Lymphedema patients can be at high risk of developing infections. Most infections develop from trauma, insect bites, injections, postoperative fluid extraction (seroma) from chest wall or axilla, or radiation dermatitis. Based on information that has been compiled over time on a case-by-case basis, these appear to be the main factors responsible for the initial onset and progression of postsurgical and other types of lymphedema.

Prevention: Patients who are properly educated in the signs and prevention of infection can ward off many debilitating, and sometimes tragic, results of recurrent infection (including subsequent increase of swelling, skin breakdown, and possible limb loss [sepsis]). Unfortunately, many patients, although well educated in proper hygiene and preventive technique, will develop chronic, idiopathic inflammations.

Signs and symptoms: The onset may vary, but often patients first notice:

a. A rash and itching on the affected limb.
b. Discoloration.
c. Increased swelling.
d. Increased temperature.
e. Heavy sensation in the limb.
f. Pain radiating in axilla.

g. Chills and a high fever, at times in a matter of five to ten minutes.

Treatment: Discontinue all treatment immediately at onset of infection (MLD, bandaging, garments). Depending upon the severity, follow the instructions below. (For some patients, rest and pushing fluids will be enough to cause the symptoms to subside, but this is only a small percentage.) Most patients will require:

a. Oral antibiotics.
b. Rest.
c. Increase fluid intake.
d. Stay out of the direct sun.
e. Watch for changes in the limb.
f. Check your temperature every six hours.

If no response to the above, the patient most likely will require hospitalization and intravenous antibiotics for several days.

As a patient, the responsibility for taking proper care of yourself is yours. Be kind to yourself, and maintain optimum health by getting plenty of rest, eating a balanced diet, drinking plenty of water, and following a well-designed exercise program.

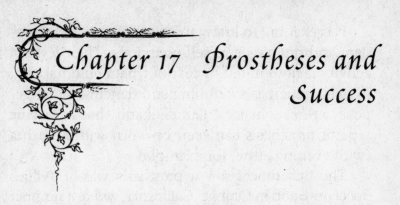

Chapter 17 *Prostheses and Success*

Although I chose reconstructive surgery, I feel it is important to acknowledge the success of prostheses. We have come a long way since cotton-formed breasts that would potentially fall out of bras and cause a woman to feel self-conscious and embarrassed. Today there is a wide selection of shapes, sizes, colors, and types of prostheses to accommodate a woman's individual needs. In addition, they are manufactured as a silicone-based product; some adhere directly to the chest wall, while others can be worn in a pocketed bra. The weight of today's prosthesis is also much lighter, which allows a woman to feel more natural and confident.

Many of the women I have spoken to say they hardly ever think about their prostheses once they have them on. Depending on a woman's choice of fit and quality, prices vary. Some insurance companies may cover a portion of the cost and allow for a new purchase every two years.

It is exciting to know that women can feel confident and no longer be self-conscious. Their level of activity is not limited by fear of what could happen. Activities such as swimming and dancing no longer pose a threat. In fact, I understand that a specific type of prosthesis can even be worn without a bra (with evening attire, for example).

The first time I saw a prosthesis was at Willie's Specialty Shop in Orange, California, where a number of women came in for fittings. I had the pleasure of meeting Willie and her daughter, Kris, two very knowledgeable and special women who went beyond the call of duty to accommodate me. I went there to get fitted for an elastic sleeve that would control the swelling in my arm. I couldn't help but notice a wonderful assortment of colorful and stylish bathing suits specifically designed for women who wore a prosthesis. On another occasion I happened to be there to rent a lymph pump when I met a woman who was trying on bathing suits. I was so impressed with how great she looked! No one would ever know she was wearing a prosthesis! It made me happy to see how at ease she was with the whole process.

The following is a personal account written by Joy Escoe, a nurse practitioner and a very happy client of Willie's.

It was wonderful—I danced at my niece's
wedding! I mean I really danced! I did the twist,

I jazzed, I hip-grinded with the rock music, and swirled around to the hora. My salmon-colored jersey dress was cut low in front and the skirt moved around as I moved to the rhythms. Everything stayed in place. The neckline didn't gape, even when I bent down to kiss an elderly aunt. Best of all, my falsie didn't leave my bra. But it wasn't always this way.

In the fall of 1976, I discovered a tumor in my right breast and underwent a mastectomy. The surgery went well, and I couldn't wait to leave the hospital. My husband brought me a loose-fitting T-shirt to wear on the trip home. I padded the right side with Kleenex over the surgical dressings. Since I couldn't wear a bra so soon after the surgery, my left breast sagged to match the mass on my right.

My husband Ben thought I looked very natural. Except for the fact that I had difficulty moving my right arm, I felt pretty normal, so we accepted a dinner invitation for that same evening. I stuffed the T-shirt, then added a cotton jacket to make the outfit look more complete and to hide the wiggle of my normal breast. We left the house on an emotional high.

Our friends welcomed us and then, remembering mid-hug that I had just had a breast removed, they became afraid to get too close. I heard people say, with undisguised surprise,

"Gee, you look wonderful." Then in the next breath, but in lowered tones, "How do you REALLY feel?"

After a round of drinks, one lady came over to me. Taking a deep breath she began to tell me that mine was the one operation she dreaded the most. She began to cry. She unloaded all of the myths that had her convinced that a woman without two breasts wasn't a woman anymore. I remember thinking, "Oh hell," and I found my-self spending the rest of the evening comforting all the women and somehow convincing the men that their wives could still be sexy even after, God forbid, a mastectomy.

It never ceases to amaze me to experience the strength and conviction that exudes from so many women who have survived this disease. It is ab-solutely astounding!

In addition to many specialty shops, some of the larger department stores such as Nordstrom carry a variety of prostheses. I recently had the honor of meeting Phyllis Clark, the Nordstrom Orange County Regional Prosthesis Coordinator. As a certified pros-thesis fitter, she assists women (by appointment) in selecting a prosthesis that best suits their needs.

In addition to this service, she has developed Nordstrom's "Making the Most of Me" (MMM) program, designed to honor breast cancer survivors and help them improve their self-image and self-esteem by simply recognizing that if patients can be helped to look good they will feel better, and the quality of their lives can improve. Each October, during Breast Cancer Awareness month, six to eight survivors are featured in a full-scale fashion event. The survivors are selected through nominations submitted by family, physicians, and breast care co-ordinators. Last fall, an audience of six hundred attended the event at Nordstrom in Riverside, California. This program is in its fourth year and has grown into a major annual corporate event for the Nordstrom Orange County Region.

Nordstrom is also the first retail store I know of that has a mammography center on-site in some of their stores. Women are given pagers to wear as they shop leisurely. Once they are paged, they are given a beautiful robe to change into, in preparation for their mammogram. In my opinion, this certainly creates an environment for women to feel truly honored.

It's women like Willie, Kris, and Phyllis—along with outstanding services that are provided through Nordstrom—that empower women to feel great about themselves, *especially* after a mastectomy!

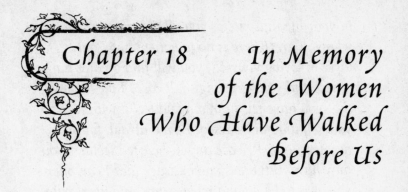

Chapter 18   In Memory of the Women Who Have Walked Before Us

It's no wonder that breast cancer is recognized as the "nice lady" disease, since so many of the women who have died are nothing short of angels *who have given so much and asked for so little.* In my own sorrow, I ask, "What can I learn from the women who have died? What is the message that they each wish to leave behind? If they had to do it all again, would anything have been changed?" Perhaps a second opinion, getting to a doctor sooner, feeling less guilt for what was really desired, and, most important, taking better care of themselves might be some of the things they might change. In many cases, their love for others was so great that it didn't take much to completely lose themselves in the heart of that love. I believe that if they could send a message, they would say something like this:

> *My love for you shall always be with you. It is not always what you do in life, but what you love*

*in your life that makes you all that you are and
who you are. There is no judgment here, only
love. In loving yourself, you will find greater happiness and your grieving shall ease. Take the love
that you have felt from me and feel it within
yourself and for yourself. Be not afraid, for you
are not alone. Release any ill-hearted feelings you
may have. If there is one message that I can offer
you, it is to let go and release any emotional pain
you may be feeling. Allow your heart to be happy
and sing your praise. This is my wish for you and
all who walk the earth plane.*

What you just read came to me at a speed that is
difficult to describe! I typed this into my computer
without even thinking, which is very unusual. Although these words are reflective of many thoughts I
have shared with you, it feels as if someone just spoke
through me. I am awestruck by the overwhelming
feeling of peacefulness that I have received from these
beautiful words. My own heart feels lighter.

The following is a loving poem written by Leslie
Goldman as a tribute to his mother, who died of
breast cancer.

IN MEMORIAM

TO ALL THE MOTHERS
I HAVE KNOWN

by Leslie Goldman

Mother, is that you calling out?
Mother, hold me in the name
of all the other wonderful mothers
I've known no longer in this world.
Hold me for the time that was sacrificed
when I put on my blue jeans,
baseball cap, and T-shirt,
took my filled lunch pail
and left the house for school.

With an empty pit in my stomach
I greet you,
as if there was so much more for me
if I just stayed home, played,
and said thank you.

Oh how I made worlds of meaning
just in bed. With one sweep
of my hands I tossed my blankets
in the air and they landed
as holy caves and mountains.

With the little plastic men you bought me
at the drug store, I worked out the entire history
and future of civilization, armies and
counterarmies,
cowboys and Indians.
In the next room, how comforting
to hear your presence.
Resting, cleaning from one Sabbath
or preparing for the next,
listening to your favorite TV program,
drinking your Maxwell House,
you did the holy acts of making a home.
What I'd trade to eat a lamb chop made by you
or sit again late night in the kitchen
while my nervousness subsided
as you helped me learn to add.

Summertime, we kids skated until
the last glimmers of light were gone.
You and Gilbert sat on the porch
philosophizing while I fell asleep.
"Gilbert, it's time to come home!"
his wife's voice would ring out from the distance.
"I'm talking to Ann!" he said,
and then there was quiet.

Mrs. Tarshes, remember her?
She was my stern teacher
who taught me to spell and read.

So fierce, she softened and turned
from a specter of discipline to my dear friend.
She was at your funeral to comfort me;
her presence so deep,
my whole being found a home for an instant
in her compassion.
How strange, my father kept her own passage
from me until years after she joined you.

Have you seen Edith, who came into my life
when I went to college?
Jon, her son, shared her with me.
She was my chance to say goodbye properly.
I was older now and knew better
the worth of precious moments.
Falling into her final sleep,
I visited her bedside and placed roses on her chest
that filled her unconscious mind.
How she loved beauty!
As her body drifted to another paradise
I told her things I knew about heaven,
things I would have answered you, Mom,
if I had only known more about living and dying.

Edith, how we danced life through
celebrating old silent movies
and made a festive occasion
of two eggs and toast.

Was it by coincidence I carried
the name of your late husband?
Praise you all, I love you dearly,
mothers of mine, so good,
so good for this world.
Pure love expressed, my old friends,
I remind myself you are not gone, and say hello.

—WINTER 1985

Chapter 19　　 *Expressions of Gratitude*

One of the greatest joys I have received throughout this journey are the many acquaintances and relationships with survivors across the country. Although I have not actually seen many of their faces, it has been an honor to listen to their hearts and hear their voices. We have shared many stories, laughed, and even cried—in some cases all in the name of gratitude; a thanksgiving and a celebration for being alive!

Every story is as unique and as beautiful as the next. Every woman I have spoken to who has survived breast cancer has an inspirational story and an expression of gratitude. Without always knowing, they have blessed the lives of many healthy women and men through example, strength, and conviction.

The following stories are written by very beautiful and powerful women. While many are survivors, I feel it is important to also acknowledge those whose lives have been incredibly inspired by survivors. This is a sampling of the many loving hearts I have met. It's voices like these that have confirmed many of my findings and remind me of my own gratitude for the insight I have received. Though none of these women have read this book, their statements contain an astonishingly similar message!

Story #1: A New Life, a New Me

It's been five years since my diagnosis of breast cancer, and it seems like yesterday and a lifetime. When I look back, I'm in awe of forces I didn't know existed then and am still learning to trust now.

My inner journey began, not with the diagnosis, but about a week and a half after my mastectomy. I was listening to a tape about healing while recuperating from surgery when I heard something that changed my life. Dr. Simonton was talking about his experience with cancer patients and said, "It's my experience that cancer patients need their cancer. They don't want it, but they need it because it's their body's way of telling them they are on the wrong path." I sat up and said, "That's me!" I had been on a path for twenty years without thinking, without feeling, and without consciously choosing. I had achieved something many people strive for: an executive position in a company I had helped build. But I wasn't happy. I was constantly doing—never *being*.

Upon hearing Dr. Simonton, I decided immediately to leave my job at the end of the year and to work part-time until then. I had no idea what I would do, but I knew it was right. While many people thought I was crazy—"What will you do for medical insurance? How will you support yourself?"—I never wavered because I was clear about my choice for the first time in my life. I visualized myself jumping off a cliff, but instead of crashing down I would soar overhead, looking at all my options, and softly land when I had determined what was right for me.

The last five years have been such a gift. I have taken up yoga and now teach it several times a week. I sold my home and rented an apartment overlooking the ocean; I find joy watching the dolphins, whales, and seals as they swim by. A year ago, I started a management consulting and seminar business out of my home, and I love the flexibility of hours and projects. Twice a year, I teach yoga and assist at Healing Odyssey, a retreat for women cancer survivors. Each time I come home with a renewed spirit. I continue to develop an awareness of my body and my emotions, and am learning to heed what they are telling me. Someone once said to me, *"Remember to fill your cup first, so that you have something left to give to others."* At last, permission to take care of me!

The biggest gift of all is the gratitude I feel, at times overwhelming, for my life and for the opportunity given to me to take the blinders off and really live. As Emmet Fox says, "Bless a thing and it will bless you. Curse it and it will curse you. If you bless a situation, it has no power to hurt you, and even if it is troublesome for a time, it will gradually fade out, if you sincerely bless it."

—BARRI CARIAN

Story #2: A Lesson in "Being"

I have been asked, "Which had the greater impact on your life? Having breast cancer or climbing Mount Aconcagua?" (a 23,000-foot mountain in Argentina that I climbed in 1995). For me it was the mountain climb. But this is because reaching the summit of the mountain marked the first anniversary of my recovery. It provided me with the distance from my diagnosis and from my everyday life to put things in perspective.

For sixteen days, my life took on an almost ascetic simplicity. I felt an essential connection with the mountain, the world, and with life. It became very clear to me what is important. What allows me to be the "human being" I want to be instead of the "human doing" I sometimes felt I had become. It was on the mountain I decided to leave the career I had pursued for more than twenty years in order to have more flexibility in my life, more time for things that are most important to me, more time to "give back" in return for the many blessings I have received.

Without breast cancer, I would not have participated in *Expedition Inspiration*. I would not have had the opportunity to climb Mount Aconcagua. I might not have discovered this important connection with my very being. Although I hope others learn this lesson about *being* without the experience of breast cancer, I'm not sure I would have. For me, the lesson was a gift that came in some pretty ugly wrapping, but one for which I am incredibly grateful.

Two years later, I am almost as busy *doing* as ever! Nonetheless, I have managed to spend more than twelve weeks backpacking, mountain climbing, and skiing. I have given countless hours to protect the environment and to my community. I have given about as many hours raising awareness and funds to fight breast cancer. I continue to work, but as an independent consultant. I try to do only work that I love to do, and only with people I love to work with.

I am not suggesting that climbing mountains is the panacea for all of life's stresses and troubles. It is not. For most people it is not even a possible pursuit. What does seem important is to take the time (or make the time) to gain perspective and take stock. Most people I know who have had breast cancer (and I know many) say the same thing. In their own words, perhaps using different metaphors, they have a new perspective on their lives, and with it have gained a sense of well-*being*.

—NANCY KNOBLE

Story #3: The Hidden Blessings

My breast cancer journey was a true "conversion experience." The indwelling of the Holy Spirit took place within the Beatitudes Prayer Community in La Mirada, California, as hands were laid on me and ten faith-filled women prayed for my healing. Through surgery and final reconstruction for bilateral mastectomy, the Lord truly was my shepherd.

With the blessing of a great prognosis, I entered into the ministry of peer support volunteering. I have counseled numerous women who learned that they have breast cancer. I share my accumulated knowledge of the disease with them as well as my heart. I try to give back what was given by the Lord to me during my journey.

Many have heard me say that if given a choice today, I would not trade away my breast cancer experience, because through it I have known the deep love of family and friends. I have a keener appreciation of what's important in my life and a very personal relationship with the Lord.

Three months after my diagnosis, I was asked to help found an Orange County Chapter of Y-ME. This has been another blessing in my life. Through our chapter, which is affectionately known as Bloomers (Breast Loss Organization Opting for Medical Education, Research, and Support), we have touched the lives of hundreds of individuals affected by breast cancer.

Having celebrated my fifth anniversary of being cancer-free, I can look back and, with a grateful heart, thank the Lord for the opportunity to trust in Him and to have received so much more than I ever would have known to ask for. "He will never forget you, for He has carved you in the palm of His hand."

—GERRY STACY
Y-ME Orange County Bloomers (California)

Story #4: Women Are Heroes

Like most women, I am strong, always taking care of my friends and family and handling life well. But not until I started working on a day-to-day basis with women who had breast cancer and subsequently developed lymphedema did I really understand the meaning of strength: to remain so tough after all they had gone through, all they had faced each day. Listening to their stories and seeing their determination to enjoy each day to the fullest has not only inspired me, but has given me more stamina, more perseverance, and more guts. These women have strengthened my belief in the goal of educating the medical community about lymphedema. They have made me even more determined to support the thousands of women who develop lymphedema after breast cancer surgery; to help them understand how to take care of themselves.

Women are emotionally strong, but the women I have followed through breast cancer seem to have found within themselves even deeper reserves. I am thinking of one patient, Pat North. She had metastatic breast cancer, but it wasn't her doctor or husband who took care of her—it was the other way around. She took care of *their* needs. She was the strong one, until one week before her death. We were on the phone together when she *finally* cried. She felt guilty because she could not cook dinner or do the dishes anymore. Pat has helped me understand what caring really means. At the same time, it has become clear to me that all of us women need to be able to let go and life will go on. We don't have to do it all and end up dying!

In April 1991 Laura Evans was referred to me for

treatment of her lymphedema. She had been told that she likely would live only a couple of years with the many positive lymph nodes she had. We both love the mountains and bonded immediately. After two months of treatment for lymphedema, while at the same time undergoing radiation treatment, she left saying, "When I feel stronger, let's climb a mountain!" Not only did this become a reality, but I was fortunate to join her and seventeen other breast cancer survivors in climbing the highest mountain in the Western Hemisphere. The time I spent on the mountain with these incredible women was something I will never forget. It has brought more faith and happiness into my life. I am proud to have been part of such a powerful group of women. No day goes by that I don't hear Laura's voice when she reached the summit. At 23,000 feet she yelled out, "We are doing this for all women with breast cancer, and we all love you!" Laura gave me a clear message to love my patients through my ongoing work in the field of lymphedema.

—Saskia R. J. Thiadens, R.N.

Story #5: Celebration of Life!

I just celebrated my fiftieth birthday. It was for me, a "celebration of life." Why was I celebrating a milestone of life that many women seem to dread? I was diagnosed with breast cancer and had a mastectomy at age thirty-four. At thirty-six, I was diagnosed with bilateral lung metastases, and with the adjunct of chemotherapy I was given a year and a half to live. The diagnosis of breast cancer and a terminal prognosis at age thirty-six definitely reframes one's perspective on life. The initial diagnosis, fear, and treatment is a struggle to conquer one day at a time. I made a conscious choice not to fulfill the prognosis and, instead, to be a part of the healing process. It was a long journey, but a hopeful and growthful one. I used meditation and visualization; I made changes in my diet and nutrition. I looked at issues causing stress in my life and made definite changes to bring *positive energy into my life*. I continued my medical treatment. The first X ray after beginning treatment showed that the masses had almost disappeared. I continued all my healing work and medical treatment. Then the last small masses totally disappeared.

The journey down the path to this special birthday has brought many lessons and many gifts. There have been many lessons about inner growth, about believing in myself, and about accepting and loving myself. The greatest lesson is that each day is a gift to celebrate. Breast cancer can be a turning point for positive change.

The gifts I cherish the most from *my fiftieth birthday* are not those wrapped in lovely paper with beautiful bows. I cherish the gift of my loving, supportive family. I cherish the gift of friendship. At the party we looked back at pictures of more than twenty to twenty-five years of friendship. Not only had our hairstyles and hair colors changed, but we had shared so much and grown so much. My friends and family had been there for me and given me their support and strength through my first mastectomy, through chemotherapy, and even through a second and third diagnosis of breast cancer and another mastectomy ten years later. Their unwavering belief in me, and belief that I would survive, gave me strength to believe in myself.

I cherish the gift of good health every day. I don't even mind the lines on my face. I have earned them. I cherish the prayer flag with my name on it carried to the top of the mountain by a fellow survivor. The beautiful friendships with other breast cancer survivors are treasured blessings in my life. I know that breast cancer can be a devastating diagnosis, but it can also be a treasured pathway to growth and appreciation of the gift of life. Now I celebrate each day!

—BARBARA SCOTT
Patient Educator, Breast Care Center;
Facilitator of the Breast Cancer Support Group
at the Breast Care Center (Orange, California)

Story #6: Making the Most of Me

Working on the "Making the Most of Me" program at Nordstrom was a turning point in my life. Working with breast cancer survivors has given my life new meaning, purpose, and sense of direction. Each one of the survivors who modeled in our show has left an imprint on my heart that will stay with me forever.

I remember hearing one of the model's stories: When this single mother of six children received her diagnosis, the news devastated her. She told me she stayed in bed, lost weight, and prepared to die. That was just six months ago. I thought, the courage she must have, to be here today to share her story with hundreds of strangers! She explained that she was still going through chemotherapy, and might not be feeling well at some of the meetings, and that she was losing her hair. She desired to feel good about herself again. I put all my effort into making this woman feel like a star. I found a wig that complemented her and gave her a high-fashion look, and dressed her in styles that captured all the attention. She said the makeover was inspirational and made her realize that she could look and feel like herself again. We hugged for a long time because I realized that life is so special, and each moment we have must be spent nurturing oneself . . . so we can give to others.

I met my first male breast cancer survivor during

one of the Making the Most of Me presentations. I had heard that a small percentage of men could get the disease but I didn't expect to meet one so soon. He shared how his bruised chest led him to the doctor, who confirmed that he had breast cancer. His laughter and outgoing personality still rings in my soul. I think of him with a smile of pride. I often wonder how many men who had a modified radical mastectomy, chemotherapy, and radiation therapy would still possess his humor and love for life. I think to myself: *That's* courage, and a great sense of self!

—PHYLLIS Y. CLARK
Orange County Regional Prosthesis Coordinator
(California)

Story #7: A Saved Life Can Save the Lives of Others

Who would I be without Breast Cancer? Where would I be without Breast Cancer? As I wrote those two sentences, I realized the words "breast cancer" were automatically capitalized. Breast cancer is important in my life.

Twelve years ago I was diagnosed with breast cancer. Today I am the director of a foundation committed to supporting breast cancer patients and educating women who are well. It is the educational element that consumes most of my professional time. I present corporate wellness programs, speaking on the importance of early detection of breast cancer. In the past nine months hundreds of men and women have heard about our Pearls of Wisdom program, designed to inspire women to follow early detection guidelines.

Twelve years ago a diagnosis of breast cancer taught me to be assertive about my life and my treatment choices. The past twelve years have allowed me to demonstrate that a diagnosis of breast cancer is not a death sentence. And having had breast cancer has allowed me to save other women's lives. What a privilege! What a challenge!

—BARBARA ANABO
Foundation Director of the Breast Care Center
(Orange, California)

Story #8: WIN Against Breast Cancer—
A Story of Hope

When I first heard the words, "Mrs. Mullen, you have breast cancer," I knew that my life was about to change forever. Little did I know at the time that the change would be for the better! When I was first diagnosed with breast cancer, I felt as though I had been hit by a freight train. After I caught my breath, I began quickly gathering as much information as possible about breast cancer and my treatment options. I decided right away that I was going to fight breast cancer head-on to the best of my abilities.

I was thirty-three years old when I was diagnosed with breast cancer in 1992. My husband and I, after ten years of marriage, had finally decided to start a family. In fact, I thought that I might be pregnant with our first child when I went into the hospital for my mastectomy and breast reconstruction.

I was very fortunate to have a surgeon who partnered with me from the beginning of my breast cancer treatment. Dr. Brad Edgerton performed immediate breast reconstruction and in a great way helped me to reconstruct my life! Our doctor-patient relationship grew into a partnership with my entire health care system (Kaiser Permanente) as we joined together to improve the quality of health care for breast cancer patients.

My husband and I did start a family, but not in the conventional sense. With incredible support from my husband Ken, and the guidance of Dr. Edgerton, the WIN (Women's Information Network) Against Breast Cancer organization was born. So began my commitment to reform breast cancer care, to find a cure for this disease by bringing more money into breast cancer research, and to be the voice for the women who can no longer be heard.

I continue to be inspired by the women I meet

who are survivors, those who are fighting for their lives, and those very dear friends who have lost their battle. I am always astounded by the stories of these women and families who have been touched by this disease. It is on their behalf that I have become such a strong advocate for improvements in the area of breast cancer.

My passion for this cause has seen its outgrowth in the WIN Against Breast Cancer organization. I am working to ensure that women have the most current information at their disposal to make informed treatment decisions, to support them, to help women partner with their health care team, to take personal responsibility for their health, and to let people know that they have a voice and can make a difference.

What started off as my worst nightmare has turned into a fairy tale. If I were given the choice to undo the fact that I ever had breast cancer, as odd as this may sound, I would not choose to do so. Breast cancer is not a death sentence; it is a wake-up call! My life has changed for the better since my diagnosis, and the work that I am able to do is both a blessing and a gift, for which I will always be grateful.

—BETSY MULLEN

(WIN ABC can be reached at (818) 332-2255; fax (818) 332-2585; e-mail: winabc@primenet.com)

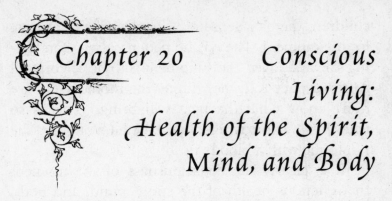

Chapter 20

Conscious Living: Health of the Spirit, Mind, and Body

The sacredness of the divine feminine spirit is with me today as waves of peacefulness wash over me. Although my work has only begun, my spirit soars as my mind fully understands the soothing elements of healing, transferred to my body. My journey will continue to unfold, no doubt. Yet this part of it comes to a splendid close.

At this moment, there is no fear, no anxiety, no guilt, no blame—only love that fills my heart. My son Christopher had whispered to me that I must come look at Arianna, who had fallen asleep. Even the most uneventful and quiet Saturdays don't guarantee that a child will voluntarily take a nap. However, today is clearly an exception. I ran upstairs to find Arianna asleep on the floor, on her side, facing Panda, a stuffed animal twice her size. Chris and I laughed quietly at the sight of this huge bear wrapping its arms around her.

When the peacefulness I feel is reflected in my

children, there's a sense of "I have arrived," at least for the moment. There is no better feeling than feeling safe and loved. This moment is to be celebrated! A friend once told me, "Enjoy the moment, for we don't know what the next will bring." This is so true. Just a short while after Arianna woke up, she ran to me with a bloody nose!

It is clearly the consciousness of the moment that offers us health of the spirit, mind, and body. When we are conscious of the expansion of the moment, really feeling and living within our heart, we find true contentment and harmony. To me, it's as though time itself does not exist, and so much more is experienced. For example, it takes far more inner strength at times to say no to guilt than it does to allow it in our lives. For me it's much like working a set of muscles I never knew I had. It takes conscious effort and persistence, since many of us have felt guilty for so many things, and for so long!

I am especially aware of my language and specific words I use. Phrases such as "to die for" or "I'm sorry" are no longer part of my daily conversation. I used to be sorry for everything, even when a particular situation didn't apply to me. Today, my sense of apology is aligned with my integrity and a stronger sense of self instead of old patterns. In other words, I consciously apologize only when I feel it is necessary. Making a conscious choice to change my ways of thinking, believing, and being is truly a commitment to the enrichment of self.

Herein lies the opportunity for others to make a similar commitment to themselves and to their loved ones, for the sake of honoring each other. I'll always remember celebrating my sixth wedding anniversary with John, and the beautiful words he spoke as he handed me a little black velvet box. As we sat together in a beachfront restaurant, I was absolutely surprised to receive this gift. He said, "I will always honor you, Stella," and I opened the box to find the most beautiful diamond and ruby ring I'd ever seen. His acknowledgment brought tears to my eyes, as it truly recognized my inner work and the process of learning to honor myself. Being honored by my husband has empowered me to take the space I need to honor myself without guilt, and in turn to honor him.

Five years have passed since then. What has been both interesting and challenging at times has been redefining how we wish to honor each other so that the other truly feels honored. For example, sometimes we base our actions on what we think will please the other person, when, in fact, it does not. This new level of awareness automatically brings all the old patterns and passed-down beliefs about relationships right into play—all the preconceptions, misconceptions, cultural beliefs, and social beliefs—

solely for the purpose of helping us learn to honor each other as man and woman.

For John and me, this has been an incredible time of redefining, reevaluating, and readjusting. Once we consciously and outwardly stated that we would honor one another, many of the old ways of being with each other that no longer served us showed up in some pretty difficult situations. Understanding that this is a process, and part of the growing pains of a relationship, is very important. This understanding has been a real breakthrough for us, and has eased the growing pains significantly.

There seems to be an unconscious expectation that the other person automatically knows how to honor you. So things sometimes seem rather disappointing at first, until there is further clarity. Since John and I choose to be conscious and do our best to communicate our needs and expectations, all the "junk" came up so we could see it, be with it, and release it! I see this process as a form of cleansing and healing. Much more about honoring one another as men and women, and relationships, is addressed in a forthcoming book as part of my *In Honor of . . .* series.

This year marks our eleventh wedding anniversary, and we are deeply grateful for all that we have learned and continue to learn. I am proud to say that the healing has transformed my life and my relationship, in large part due to an expanded and higher consciousness of being. A willingness to live consciously (in a constant state of awareness while looking for the gifts in life) is, in my opinion, what offers us health and a true sense of well-being.

Chapter 21

The Gift of "Being"

by John P. Crawley Jr.

Every man whose wife, mother, or daughter is diagnosed with breast cancer experiences a feeling of helplessness. As men, we live in a place of doing, providing, and protecting. I was stunned when Stella was diagnosed. My thoughts were: What do I say? How do I act? How can I help?

I was at her side for all of her appointments and treatments, offering my support. Yet I experienced inner conflict and frustration based on wanting to accomplish something more. I found it awkward to sit as a spectator or observer, feeling unclear about what my role involved. I know she felt stronger with my presence, but I felt constrained.

Being there just didn't seem to be enough, because my definition of "being" needed to be redefined. I felt I had to be *doing* something while I was *being* at her side. At the time I didn't realize that my simply *being* was the greatest gift I could give her.

I clearly remember sitting with Stella in the

recovery room after one of her surgeries. In the bed next to us was an elderly woman who had just had a lumpectomy. Her husband was at her side when the surgeon informed her that it was cancer. I immediately related to her husband's unconscious reaction. He tried to show a look of strength, yet he could not hide his feeling of helplessness. His face vividly reflected his feeling of inability to do anything. This experience led me to reflect on my own feelings of anger and fear, and the sense of extreme discomfort and wanting to "take on" this threat to my family. I realized at that moment how paralyzed I had felt.

My gift of learning how to *be* came, ironically, during Stella's healing process. We had more fun during her chemotherapy treatments. All worries and everyday pressures were thrown out. We didn't care about how much money we had or what we had to do. We just enjoyed being and having fun. We played more, we laughed more, and we loved more. It wasn't until after she had completed all of the treatments that I started to fall back into doing.

I started working more, and wanted to get our life back to "normal." But something was missing. Life didn't feel the same. "Normal" didn't feel normal. What was missing? We started to feel the tensions of everyday life.

One night Stella looked at me and said I didn't look happy. How could I not be happy? My wife

beat cancer. My children are beautiful and healthy.
But she was right: I was not happy. We talked about
how much fun we had had when she was going
through chemo. It was then we realized I had gone
back to doing. I wasn't being! That's when I looked
at my life and what made me happy.

How I learned to *be* was by honoring myself.
Taking time for myself, in meditation, makes a significant difference in my life. Walking, reading, and,
most important, enjoying the moment. Life is much
more enjoyable when I do what I like, and when I
am with the people I love.

I hope my account will help men feel less alone
while addressing the needs of a woman faced with a
diagnosis of cancer.

While Stella was developing this book, we shared
many stories about the issues that couples face. One
issue that is usually not discussed publicly is the
loss of the breast and its impact on the relationship.
I appreciate a woman's breasts as much as any other
man. But when Stella was diagnosed and faced with
the mastectomies, I never once thought about how I
would feel about her after the surgeries. My fear was
losing my wife and my children's mother—not her
breasts!

I've heard some sad stories of women who dress
in the dark and are afraid to show their mates the
scars of healing. Frankly, I know of no man who

would stop loving his wife because she lost a breast. Real love is about the beauty of the spirit, not the beauty of physical appearance. Long-term and life-long relationships are about loving each other's inner being.

It would seem that if the physical is most important to the man, then he does not belong in that relationship. But the woman must let him decide. *Don't make the decision for him!* Sometimes it takes the threat of losing someone you love to recognize your depth of love for this being. With this recognition, your partner will look more beautiful than ever! I feel that most men need to express this more often, and most women need to hear it more often.

My message to the husbands, fathers, brothers, and sons of women who face this challenge: *Be* there! Hold her hand, share your feelings, look into the eyes that you love so much, and she'll know you're there. That's all she needs . . . your smile, your love, and your *being* there.

God bless you all.

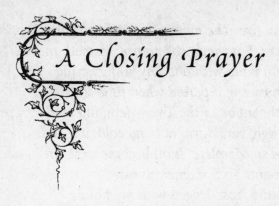

A Closing Prayer

I am grateful to conclude this book with a prayer that exemplifies the passion that comes with self-realization and self-acknowledgment. These words declare a new level of consciousness. This prayer reflects the cleansing, healing, strength, and balance that we each own as a result of our awakening to honor the divine feminine and masculine within.

Father, husband, and spiritual healer, Pindey Shahi shares his loving energy as closure for this book. The prayer was inspired by a dream he had on the same day that he bid farewell to a special friend who died of breast cancer, which was the very day he delivered it to me.

THE FLAME AND THE WATER

*The embankment of the pond was ablaze
with a fierce fire. The intensity of the fire must
have shaken me out of that dream. My chest felt*

like it was on fire. The memories came rushing as I laid there. But there was no fire; instead, the most tranquil pond with one tiny, unflickering flame. Memories of a period when time stood still, when the union of the Two—feminine and masculine, light and dark, hot and cold, life and death—was so complete. It all became so clear in that moment. That moment is now.

I am sitting cross-legged with my hands folded. My God reality is looking at me, into my eyes, and saying:

I am the Giver and the Receiver.
I am the Love and the Loved.
I am the Feminine and the Masculine.
I am the Honor and the Honored.
I am the Flame and the Water.

—PINDEY SHAHI

Resources

American Cancer Society (ACS)
   (800) ACS-2345
Known as the nationwide community-based voluntary health organization dedicated to eliminating cancer as a major health problem by preventing cancer, saving lives, and diminishing suffering from cancer through research, education, advocacy, and service.

BIONUTRITIONAL CONSULTANTS
(John P. Rodino, Ph.D.)
   10900 Warner
   Suite 203
   Fountain Valley, CA 92708
   (714) 962-0676
John P. Rodino, Ph.D., is a biochemical analyst with a unique background in biochemical research, development, and education. His pioneering efforts of twenty years helped spearhead the use of prostaglandins, enzymes, and protein—which are widely used today. His techniques of

evaluating blood chemistries to design nutritional programs support healing for people in health crisis.

Kaylim Laboratories
    634 North Poplar Street
    Suite A
    Orange, CA 92868
    (800) 778-1171
    fax: (714) 634-4146
Established in 1983, Kaylim Laboratories has been dedicated to provide nutritional products to treat people's diverse nutritional needs. Products such as Genopro High Protein Powder and other fine products. Our goal is to help people to live a healthier life and to build a healthier body.—Pres. John P. Rodino Jr.

The National Alliance of Breast Cancer
Organizations (NABCO)
    9 East 37th Street, 10th Floor
    New York, NY 10016
    (800) 719-9154
    fax: (212) 689-1213
Established in 1986, this is the leading nonprofit central resource for information about and assistance with breast cancer, offering up-to-date, accurate information to the media, medical organizations, and professionals; and a network of more than 375 organizations that provide detection, treatment, and care to hundreds of thousands of women. In addition, NABCO spends time

locally, on the state level, and in Washington, DC,
advocating regulatory change and legislation to benefit
breast cancer patients. Benefits of membership include
NABCO News, a quarterly update, and the annual
Breast Cancer Resource List.

National Cancer Institute (NCI)
   (800) 4-CANCER
*The leading national agency for research on the causes,
prevention, early detection, diagnosis, and treatment of
cancer. The mission of the NCI is scientific discovery
about all aspects of cancer toward the ultimate
elimination of cancer from our lives. The research
programs of the NCI take place in three complementary
settings: the laboratory, the clinic, and the community.
The Cancer Information Service (CIS) is a program of the
National Cancer Institute that provides a nationwide
telephone service for cancer patients and their families
and friends, the public, and health professionals.*

National Lymphedema Network (NLN)
   2211 Post Street, Suite 404
   San Francisco, CA 94115
   (415) 921-1306
   National Hotline: (800) 541-3259
   home page: www.hooked.net/~lymphnet
*An internationally recognized nonprofit organization that
provides education and support about lymphedema
prevention, treatment, and research to patients, health care*

professionals, and the general public. The NLN provides an 800 hotline, on-line home page, and quarterly newsletter that includes a resource guide, PenPals, features, and cutting-edge articles on current issues in lymphedema.

Northwest Lymphedema Center
    1800 NW Market Street, Suite 203B
    Seattle, WA 98107-3908
    (888) 200-8002
    (206) 782-5598
    fax: (206) 782-2079
"Helping others understand and meet the challenges of lymphedema." A 501c(3) nonprofit service organization providing information, resources, and referrals for lymphedema patients and their families. Active since 1993, Northwest Lymphedema Center volunteers hold monthly support group meetings that focus on empowering patients through education and self-care classes. Donations, dues, and proceeds from sales of self-help videos sustain a quarterly newsletter and provide compression garments and bandages for patients who are unable to pay for these items.

Susan G. Komen Breast Cancer Foundation
    5005 LBJ Freeway, Suite 370
    Dallas, TX 75244
    (800) IM-AWARE [(800) 462-9273]
    (972) 385-5000

fax: (972) 385-5005

home page: www.breastcancerinfo.com

*Established in 1982, this nonprofit organization has a
network of volunteers, working through local chapters
and Race for the Cure® events across the country, fighting
to eradicate breast cancer as a life-threatening disease.
In addition to funding national research grants, Komen
funds education, screening, and treatment projects in
communities across the country, and delivers the life-
saving message of early detection to hundreds of
thousands of men and women. Call for more information
regarding breast health or breast cancer concerns.*

Women's Information Network (WIN) Against
Breast Cancer

19325 E. Navilla Place

Covina, CA 91723-3244

(818) 332-2255

fax: (818) 332-2585

e-mail: winabc@primenet.com

*This nonprofit organization provides information
on breast health and wellness, and breast cancer
treatment options, support, and research to patients
and their families, survivors, the health care
community, and other groups throughout the country.
WIN-ABC is committed to providing patients from
all socioeconomic backgrounds rapid access to
comprehensive, state-of-the-art support and education,*

including a free in-depth resource guide, through the
Breast Aid® Breast Buddy® program, the signature
program that has brought WIN-ABC into the forefront
of patient advocacy organizations throughout the
United States.

Y-ME National Breast Cancer Organization
    (800) 221-2141
*Established in 1978, this nonprofit, consumer-oriented
organization provides information, referrals, and
emotional support to individuals concerned about or
diagnosed with breast cancer. Its national toll-free
hotline is staffed by trained volunteers and staff who
have experienced breast cancer. Men whose partners
have experienced breast cancer and Spanish-speaking
counselors are also available. A wig and prosthesis bank
is available for those in need.*

My Personal Journal

_____

_____

_____

_____

_____

_____

_____

_____

_____

_____

_____

_____

_____

_____

_____

_____

_____

My Personal Journal

_____

_____

_____

_____

_____

_____

_____

_____

_____

_____

_____

_____

_____

_____

_____

_____

My Personal Journal

_____

_____

_____

_____

_____

_____

_____

_____

_____

_____

_____

_____

_____

_____

_____

My Personal Journal

_____

_____

_____

_____

_____

_____

_____

_____

_____

_____

_____

_____

_____

_____

_____

My Personal Journal

_____

_____

_____

_____

_____

_____

_____

_____

_____

_____

_____

_____

_____

_____

_____

_____

My Personal Journal

_____

_____

_____

_____

_____

_____

_____

_____

_____

_____

_____

_____

_____

_____

_____

My Personal Journal

_____

_____

_____

_____

_____

_____

_____

_____

_____

_____

_____

_____

_____

_____

My Personal Journal

_____

_____

_____

_____

_____

_____

_____

_____

_____

_____

_____

_____

_____

_____

_____

_____

_____

My Personal Journal

_____

_____

_____

_____

_____

_____

_____

_____

_____

_____

_____

_____

_____

_____

_____

My Personal Journal

_____

_____

_____

_____

_____

_____

_____

_____

_____

_____

_____

_____

_____

_____

My Personal Journal

_____

_____

_____

_____

_____

_____

_____

_____

_____

_____

_____

_____

_____

_____

_____

My Personal Journal

_____

_____

_____

_____

_____

_____

_____

_____

_____

_____

_____

_____

_____

_____

_____

_____

My Personal Journal

_____

_____

_____

_____

_____

_____

_____

_____

_____

_____

_____

_____

_____

_____

_____

_____

_____

My Personal Journal

My Personal Journal

_____

_____

_____

_____

_____

_____

_____

_____

_____

_____

_____

_____

_____

_____

My Personal Journal

_____

_____

_____

_____

_____

_____

_____

_____

_____

_____

_____

_____

_____

_____

_____

_____

_____

My Personal Journal

_____

_____

_____

_____

_____

_____

_____

_____

_____

_____

_____

_____

_____

_____

_____

_____

_____

My Personal Journal

About the Author

STELLA TOGO CRAWLEY was diagnosed with breast cancer at age thirty-two. Her interviews with more than 200 breast cancer survivors revealed that "giving too much" is a common thread. An author, speaker, and consultant, Crawley is dedicated to helping women relearn the lost art of receiving. She currently lives with her husband and two children in California, where she is working on a series of *In Honor of . . .* books.

115 - gathering of women, 120
Being with someone facing lifethreat 118
119, 120, 143-44

To forward your communications to the author, write to:

Stella Togo Crawley
PO Box 99
Yorba Linda, CA 92885-0099